The DIY Bathroom Book

GW00362423

The DIY Bathroom Book

Roger DuBern

Illustrations by David Papworth
Electrics section by Geoffrey Burdett

Newnes Technical Books

Newnes Technical Books
is an imprint of the Butterworth Group
which has principal offices in
London, Boston, Durban, Singapore, Sydney, Toronto,
Wellington

First published 1984

British Library Cataloguing in Publication Data

DuBern, Roger
 The DIY bathroom book.
 1. Bathrooms – Remodelling – Amateurs' manuals
 I. Title
 643'.52   TH4816

 ISBN 0-408-01339-7

Library of Congress Cataloging in Publication Data

DuBern, Roger.
 The DIY bathroom book.

 Includes index.
 1. Bathrooms.   2. Dwellings – Remodelling.
 3. Do-it-yourself work.
 I. Title   II. Title: The D.I.Y. bathroom book.
 TH6485.D83   1984   643'.52   83-23756
 ISBN 0-408-01339-7 (U.S.)

Typeset by Butterworths Litho Preparation Department
Printed in Scotland by Blantyre Printing & Binding Co. Ltd.,
Glasgow

Preface

Contents

Attitudes towards the British bathroom have changed dramatically in recent years. And what used so often to be a cold, clinical in-and-out room has developed into an attractive, cosy place to be.

And yet the bathroom still seems to be the poor relation of many a home, and if this your experience, the author offers you plenty of practical advice to help you transform yours, whether it needs redecorating, refurbishing or a total change of layout.

Choice of the right materials to use can be a problem in this room of high humidities and constant changes of temperature, and the author calls upon his considerable personal experience to help you choose.

The term do-it-yourself encompasses a very wide range of activities, and you will find other books in this series to help you with specific areas of activity. All have been written by people with considerable DIY experience, used to dealing with readers' enquiries, so they approach their subjects in a very practical down-to-earth manner.

I am sure you will find their help invaluable, and I wish you every success in your DIY activities.

Tony Wilkins
Executive Editor, Do-it-yourself Magazine

Introduction

In many houses the bathroom tends to get treated like the Cinderella of pantomime fame. While other rooms in the house are improved and redecorated, the bathroom is often left more or less as found, except perhaps for the addition of some new wall tiles and a coat of paint. At best, it is probably the last room in the house that does come in for major improvement.

While many people are quite prepared to tackle other important renovation work around the house, and even to take on ambitious projects like fitting a completely new kitchen, there seems to be an in-built reluctance by many home-owners to update their bathroom. And as for installing completely new washing and toilet facilities, say in a second bathroom, in a bedroom or in a new cloakroom, this is almost taboo!

It is hard to understand this reluctance when so often the new facilities are sorely needed, when the cost is likely to be a lot less than many people are prepared to spend on a new kitchen, and when the cost of the work is almost certain to more than pay for itself by adding to the value of the house when the property comes to be sold.

Perhaps the reason is fear! Fear of the unknown, because in the past plumbing was a trade surrounded by mystery: the roaring blowlamp, wiped soldered joints, and much muttering coming from behind the bath panels as the tradesman went about his work. There is also the fear in many people's minds that the whole job could get out of hand and turn into a traumatic experience. The possibility of the place being flooded with water, for example, or the lavatory being out of use for several days, could be enough to put off the faint-hearted.

However, as this book will show, such fears are unfounded, and if the work is carried out methodically as explained in the following chapters, any reasonably competent DIYer will be able to install a new bathroom with virtually no trouble at all. And the work need not take long either. If the job involves simply changing out-of-date bathroom fittings for the latest styles, then it is perfectly feasible to have the new fittings installed and working in a weekend. The WC pan need be out of use only for 30 minutes! Also, there is no need to worry about smells and general unpleasantness associated with changing a lavatory pan, because if you tackle this in the right way as explained in this book, and use the latest flexible pan connectors, the job is by no means as bad as you may imagine.

When it comes to choosing the bathroom equipment and plumbing fittings that will be required, everything is being done to help the DIY installer. At the major bathroom and kitchen improvement centres and at DIY superstores you can see displays of all the latest equipment, and in most cases there are self-service racks so that you can spend as much time as you like looking for the right fittings even if you are not familiar with their trade names. Of course, ideally the store will also have qualified staff on hand with experience in fitting bathrooms, and these people should be prepared to answer your questions and make helpful suggestions regarding the best fittings to use for any particular circumstances.

One way to make selection easier is to choose a packaged bathroom unit where all the matching fittings are supplied in a plastic shrink-wrapped package complete with bath, basin, WC pan and cistern, taps, waste outlets, toilet seats, and so on. Some manufacturers also produce really detailed and useful fitting instructions with each of their bathroom fittings, and this sort of information is something to look for when selecting the fittings. Although this book contains enough general information to enable you to fit your new bathroom, such detailed instructions for the particular fittings you have chosen will be invaluable.

Of course, an important part of fitting a new bathroom is plumbing-in the water supply and waste systems. Here, modern pipe fittings mean that the actual task of making the connections is very easy, so there is no need to have fears of getting water leaks from supply- or waste-pipe joints.

Time out of use

If you did have any doubts, with any luck by now you are thinking that you could tackle the job. But perhaps there is still just that nagging doubt that the bathroom will be out of use for longer than you think.

Well, obviously the time the job will take depends on whether there are other washing or toilet facilities in the house and whether the modernisation consists simply of the direct replacement of one bathroom fitting for the equivalent modern type, or whether the plan is to alter the layout of the bathroom, changing the positions of the fittings and adding new ones, and perhaps also carrying out structural alterations, such as building new stud walls and moving door positions.

If the bathroom has the only lavatory in the house, then the work obviously has to be planned around this fact and the time between removing the old lavatory pan and fitting the new pan has to be minimal. In fact, as mentioned previously, as long as the soil-pipe position is not moved you should be able to take out the old WC pan and fit the new pan within 30 minutes if the connection is on an upper floor where the pan will be screwed down to the timber floorboards. A couple of hours will be plenty of time to replace a

downstairs WC pan where the old pan is likely to be bedded into a solid floor which may have to be made good with quick-setting cement and where the outlet of the old WC may be cemented into a stoneware soil pipe. Once the new WC pan is in place it can be used if necessary, although in this case it will have to be flushed with buckets of water until the new cistern is connected.

Where old bathroom fittings are being replaced by new ones, you should be able to have the old fittings out and the new ones installed in a weekend, especially if you have a helper. Obviously it will be better if you can encourage the family to stay with friends or relatives for this weekend, which will enable you to crack on with the work with few interruptions.

If the house has another lavatory and if washing can be temporarily undertaken elsewhere, such as at the kitchen sink, then of course your problems are eased and the work can be undertaken at a relatively steady pace. In this case, the time the job takes will depend on the scope of any alterations and the amount of building work planned. The installation of the fittings will again take about two days if the old fittings are being changed for new ones of the same type, but allow one or two days extra if new facilities are being added, such as a separate shower or bidet. And then, of course, you have to add on extra time for any building work, such as building partition walls, raised floors, and so on.

To ensure that the work keeps to a timetable, the various jobs should be undertaken in the stages suggested in the sequence of work tables on page 51 which lists the operations in the most logical way to ensure that the work goes smoothly and easily.

To make life easier while the conversion work is being done, it is essential to cut off the water supply to the bathroom, while maintaining a supply to the rest of the house. In particular, it is essential to keep a mains cold water supply to the kitchen sink so that drinking water can be drawn, kettles can be filled for hot water, and buckets filled for flushing the lavatory if the pan has to be used before the new cistern has been connected.

Household water system

It helps to understand the layout of the household plumbing system so that water can be turned off to the bathroom and the system partially drained down without affecting the heating system nor the water supply to other parts of the house. Ideally gate valves should be fitted as shown. Alternatively the supply pipes can be sawn through and temporarily fitted with blanking plugs or stop ends until the new pipework can be connected

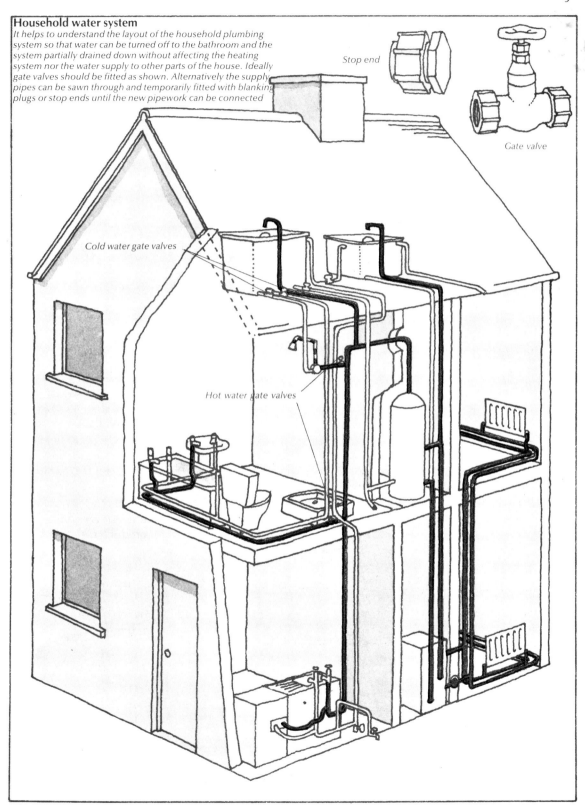

Stop end

Gate valve

Cold water gate valves

Hot water gate valves

Ideally there will be two gatevalves controlling the hot and cold water supplies to the bathroom. If these are not available it could be an idea to fit them before undertaking any work on the new bathroom. Such gatevalves will prove invaluable in the future any time it is necessary to undertake maintenance work on the bathroom fittings, such as when it is necessary to change the washers on the taps.

If there are not any gatevalves, and you do not want to fit them, an easy way to isolate the bathroom is to saw through the hot and cold water supply pipes close to the point where they enter the bathroom and temporarily fit each pipe with a blanking plug, which will only take a couple of minutes using compression fittings. Remember, though, to isolate and drain the supply pipes before sawing through them!

Tool kit

By doing it yourself you will be saving a lot of money, so use some of the savings to buy an adequate number of tools that will enable you to do the work quickly and successfully.

Probably all the standard household tools will be needed at some stage of the work, but in addition you will need a few specialist plumbing tools, such as a basin spanner and pipe-bending springs. The latter are useful for making single shallow bends in 15 mm pipe (equivalent to the old ½ in size) and 22 mm (the old ¾ in) size. You need one spring for each size. However, bending 22 mm pipe in particular takes some effort so it is well worth considering hiring a small, lightweight hand-held pipe-bending tool, such as the Handybender, which is available for hire from hire shops. In fact, these shops have available a wide selection of tools for daily or weekly hire at quite moderate rates, so it could be better to hire the specialized tools required rather than buy them. Whether to buy or hire depends on how much plumbing you intend to do in the future.

The following list gives the tools and materials that will enable you to tackle a bathroom installation.

Hacksaw
Pipe cutter (handy, but not essential)
Basin wrench
Large adjustable spanner
Cap nut spanner (for compression plumbing fittings)
Pliers or self-grip wrench
Small half-round file (for removing burrs from pipes)
Blowtorch (for capillary joints)
Paste flux (as above)
Solder (as above)
Wire wool (for cleaning tube)
Emery cloth (for cleaning tube)
Heatproof cloth (to protect walls, etc. when soldering)
PTFE tape (for waterproof connections on screwed fittings)
Plumbers' mastic (for bedding wastes, etc.)
Hammer – large (for breaking bath, WC, etc.)
Cold chisel (as above)
Bolster chisel (removal of ceramic tiles, etc.)
Pipe-bending tool (can be hired)
Pipe-bending springs – 15 mm and 22 mm (as alternatives to the above)
Screwdrivers – single slot and cross head
Drill – electric or hand (for making fixings to walls, etc.)
Masonry drill bit (as above)
Wallplugs (as above)
Trimming knife
Painting and decorating tools
Flexible steel tape
General repair and maintenance tools for specific jobs (e.g. electrician's screwdriver for wiring up)

This tool kit will enable you to plumb-in in a new bathroom. To finish off the conversion, general DIY and decorating tools will also be required. Note that alternative basin wrenches are shown, and the Stilson and Footprint wrenches are useful optional tools. You will probably not need an adjustable spanner if you have a proprietary cap nut spanner. In addition to plumber's mastic, a jointing compound, such as Boss White, can be useful when making compression joints

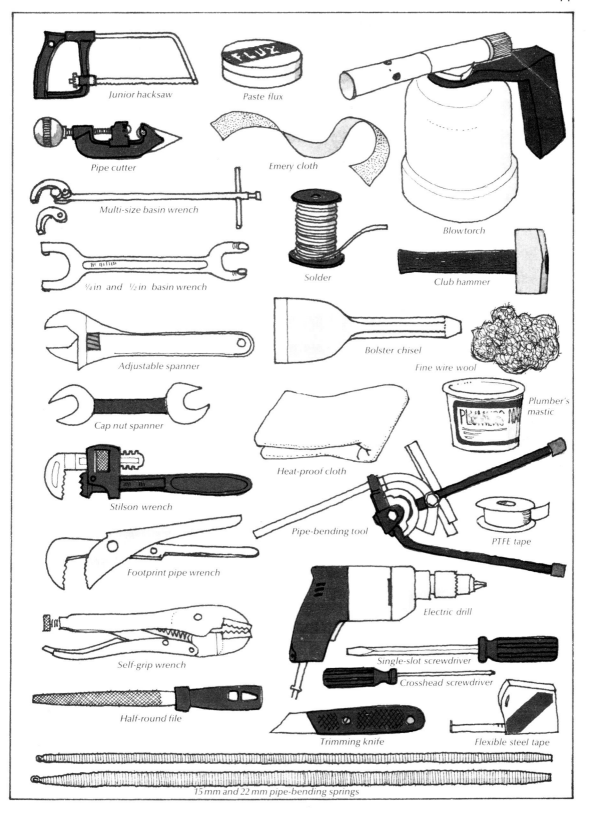

Junior hacksaw

Paste flux

Pipe cutter

Emery cloth

Blowtorch

Multi-size basin wrench

Solder

Club hammer

¼ in and ½ in basin wrench

Adjustable spanner

Bolster chisel

Fine wire wool

Cap nut spanner

Heat-proof cloth

Plumber's mastic

Stilson wrench

Pipe-bending tool

PTFE tape

Footprint pipe wrench

Electric drill

Self-grip wrench

Single-slot screwdriver

Crosshead screwdriver

Half-round file

Trimming knife

Flexible steel tape

15 mm and 22 mm pipe-bending springs

Planning

Bathroom planning involves making a number of decisions that are interrelated. It is necessary to decide what you want from the bathroom, what new fittings you would like to incorporate, whether you want to enlarge the bathroom, or make a second bathroom elsewhere.

Unfortunately, you will have to temper your ideas with what is practicably possible. There is the question of the cost of all the fittings and the decor you would like to have, plus the practical difficulties of placing the fittings exactly where you would like them. As we shall see, in practice it is important to keep the limitations of the existing drainage system in mind and plan the positions of the new fittings so they will be comparatively easy to connect up.

So take a step at a time. Take stock of what you have got at present, see how you could improve or extend, and keep the constraints of the drainage system in mind. Only when you have assessed all these points can you prepare your detailed plan.

Start by taking a long, hard look at the existing bathroom to see if the fittings are placed to the best advantage, and to find out if it is not possible to add some other facilities, such as a separate shower cubicle or a bidet. At this very early stage you will probably be able to decide very quickly, just by looking critically at the room, whether there is scope for altering or adding to the facilities that already exist.

Smaller bathroom

Obviously it is with the smaller bathroom where you need to pay the most attention to planning and really keep your wits about you if you are to fill the space to maximum advantage. This goes not only for the arrangement of the fittings, but also for the various other accessories that are needed in the bathroom such as towel rails, a medicine chest, a shower socket, mirror and so on. Of course, it is not just a question of cramming everything in. You must be able to use the equipment, and this means leaving an adequate space around each unit. It is more or less a question of commonsense regarding how much space to leave, but if you want to be sure there is enough user space, the minimum requirements are detailed on page 22, at which stage the initial planning will have been done and the final layout plans will be in the process of being drawn up.

It is important to try as far as possible to plan the new bathroom in the most practical as well as the most efficient layout. This means making a note of existing window and door positions and trying to keep them in these positions as far as possible. Obviously it is reasonably easy to re-hang a door, from say left-hand opening to right-hand. It is also quite easy to change a hinged door to one which slides. But structural alterations, such as changing the position of a door or window opening or enlarging a window can be expensive or, if you do it yourself, very time-consuming.

With regard to the plumbing arrangement, again it is important to try to plan the new layout around the positions of the existing pipes, particularly the large-diameter soil pipes and stacks which are tricky, time-consuming, and hence expensive to move. The smaller water-supply pipes are not a problem and are easily moved or extended as necessary. To understand your drainage system, see pages 15 and 16. The very simplest plumbing arrangement is to keep all the fittings along one wall, and in this way it is also very easy to keep the installation neat by boxing-in the pipework, and perhaps creating useful storage cupboards at the same time. However, if pipes are boxed-in be careful to lag them properly, since this will prevent condensation forming on cold water pipes, and will reduce heat loss from hot water pipes.

Sometimes it is reasonably easy to enlarge a small bathroom. Knocking down a wall to bring an adjacent WC into the total bathroom area can boost space remarkably and allow several new washing facilities to be included in the overall plan.

If an airing cupboard is encroaching into a small bathroom it should be possible to resite the hot water cylinder and airing cupboard in a bedroom, or on the landing, for example. It may even be worth changing the hot water heating system to an instantaneous gas or electric water-heating system, or changing it to an open-outlet electric water heater storage system. With both systems a hot water cylinder is not required and if a warm airing cupboard for linen is wanted, one of these can be installed almost anywhere with a fixed low-wattage electric tubular heater to provide the airing facilities.

Larger bathroom

At the other extreme is the large bathroom, where the problems are totally different. Here it will not be a question of trying to squeeze everything in, but rather a problem of making sure that the space is utilised properly. To anyone with a modern house it seems ridiculous to think that a bathroom could be too big, but large bathrooms are not solely the products of fantasy to be seen in the brochures of the bathroom-fitting manufacturers. Large bathrooms are very often found in old properties which were very likely built without a bathroom, but then at a later date had one of the bedrooms converted into a bathroom.

In these cases it looks ridiculous to have just two or three fittings dotted around the walls with acres of floor space between them. You can spend as much money as you like on the

fittings themselves and on the floor-covering, and the result will still be a bare, bleak and unwelcoming bathroom. With a big bathroom you need to think big to come up with eye-catching ways to install fittings in such a way that they fill the room and break it up into a number of attractive smaller units. Obviously there is a chance to have an island bath and the full range of fittings, such as double-bowl washbasins, bidet, shower enclosure, and so on. You could even have a keep-fit area, with an exercise bike or a rowing machine, or perhaps a sun bed or even a sauna cabin. The brochures of the bathroom-fitting manufacturers can be very helpful when it comes to giving ideas for larger bathrooms.

Alternatively, you could decide that it would be more practical to divide a large bathroom into two, perhaps creating a smaller room that could form an en-suite bathroom to an adjacent bedroom.

New facilities

Following the preliminary inspection of the bathroom, it is time to turn your attention to other parts of the house to see if there are any bathroom facilities that could be added elsewhere in the house to relieve the early-morning congestion that is a feature of many one-bathroom houses.

It may be possible to make a second bathroom or shower room upstairs, or even to put a vanity unit or shower cubicle into one or more of the bedrooms. It is surprising just where a shower cabinet will fit. It would not look unattractive in the corner of a bedroom, but ideally it could be built-in at the end of a row of fitted wardrobes with the wardrobe doors to completely hide the shower when not it use. There are also folding shower/wash basin units for bedrooms where space is really tight. Another often unused space where a shower cabinet could go is at the end of a landing, perhaps close to the stair well. It might not be as easy to arrange the discharge of the waste pipe here as it would be in a bedroom, especially if the cabinet is on an outside wall, but the problem should not be insurmountable.

It also pays to search out the possibilities of installing extra washing facilities downstairs. There may be space for a small cloakroom or shower cabinet downstairs – even an understair cupboard may be suitable for conversion to a cloakroom with WC and small hand wash basin, or it could house a shower cubicle. Alternatively, there may be room in the hall for those facilities or in a laundry or utility room.

Even in a basement it is possible to have a WC if a small-bore system, such as the Saniflo, is installed. This is an electrically-operated pumped system in which the waste from the WC is discharged through a 22 mm (¾ in) pipe. Not only will the system pump 2 m vertically but it pumps up to 20 m horizontally, making it very easy to install WC facilities anywhere in the house.

A home extension, whether built as a single-storey or two-storey extension, could be used partly to form a new bathroom, or perhaps by forming a new bedroom it could release an existing bedroom for conversion to a bathroom.

Perhaps part of a porch extension could be built as a small cloakroom, or it may be possible to convert part of an integral garage.

Finally, there is the loft where a new bedroom with a bathroom could be combined or, yet again, perhaps two bedrooms could be formed, releasing a bedroom elsewhere for conversion to a bathroom. There are quite a few possibilities when you think about it!

Drainage system

The existing drainage system is of considerable importance in bathroom and WC planning because it can be tricky, time-consuming, and often expensive to move or install new drains, particularly the large-diameter soil pipes and stacks which carry the waste from WCs. Waste pipes from other bathroom fittings such as washbasins, shower trays and baths, are not so difficult to move, extend or install, but as they are closely associated with soil pipes, the two need to be considered together.

Whenever possible the new fittings should be kept close to the existing soil- and waste-pipe positions so that these pipes can be reused. Alternatively, the waste from the new fittings may be fairly easily discharged into a convenient inspection chamber which may already be taking waste from another part of the house.

If the new bathroom is built a long way from the existing drains, it may be very difficult to connect the fittings to the sewer, and in this case it is best to consult the local authority building-control officer, an architect, or a builder.

With modern push-fit plastic above- and below-ground drainage systems it is possible to lay new drains, but in order to do so it is important to understand how your particular drainage system works.

In older houses (built before the 1950s) it is common to have a two-pipe drainage system. In this case the outflow from WCs (called 'soil') is kept separate from the outflow or 'waste' from baths, basins and sinks. The soil and waste pipes are run on the outside of the house (as illustrated opposite) and they meet up in an inspection chamber before they are carried in a single underground drain to the main sewer under the road.

In newer houses, single-stack drainage is used. In this case there is a single soil stack, almost invariably in a duct inside the house, and branches are taken from the stack to connect to the WC soil pipe and basin, bath and sink wastes (see diagram on page 16).

Generally speaking, installing new bathroom fittings presents few difficulties regarding waste fittings where a modern plastic waste system is used, but connecting a new WC can be more difficult. If the bathroom is in a new extension some distance from the existing drains, it may be necessary to lay a new drain from a suitable inspection chamber and this drain will have to be connected to a new soil stack which ideally will be inside the extension, but can, if necessary, be fixed outside the building.

If the new bathroom is fairly close to the existing drainage system it should not be too difficult to modify it. With a two-pipe system it should be quite easy to run the waste pipes from the new bath, basin or shower to discharge over

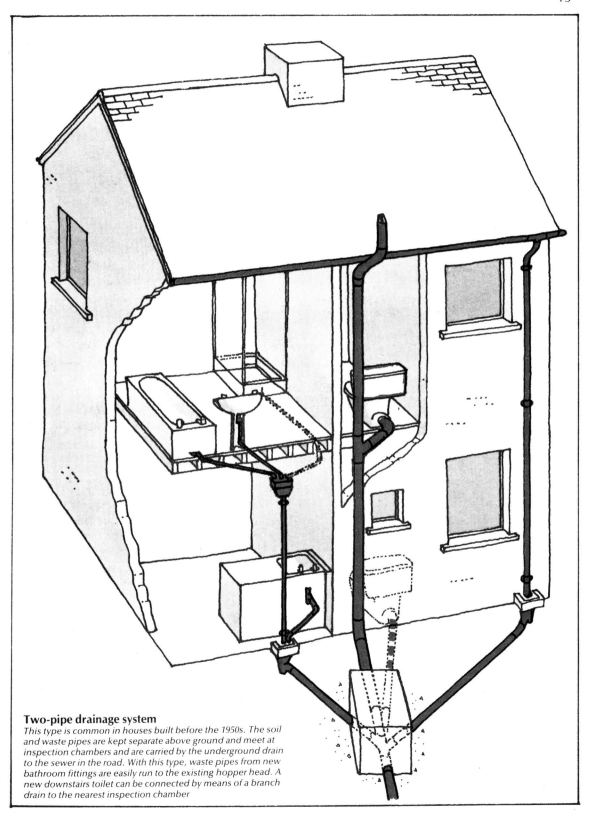

Two-pipe drainage system

This type is common in houses built before the 1950s. The soil and waste pipes are kept separate above ground and meet at inspection chambers and are carried by the underground drain to the sewer in the road. With this type, waste pipes from new bathroom fittings are easily run to the existing hopper head. A new downstairs toilet can be connected by means of a branch drain to the nearest inspection chamber

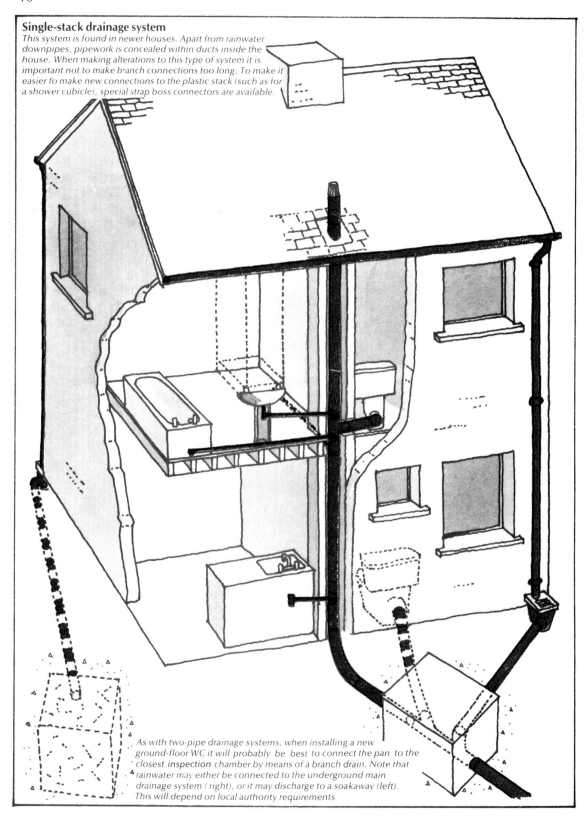

Single-stack drainage system
This system is found in newer houses. Apart from rainwater downpipes, pipework is concealed within ducts inside the house. When making alterations to this type of system it is important not to make branch connections too long. To make it easier to make new connections to the plastic stack (such as for a shower cubicle), special strap boss connectors are available.

As with two-pipe drainage systems, when installing a new ground-floor WC it will probably be best to connect the pan to the closest *inspection* chamber by means of a branch drain. Note that rainwater may either be connected to the underground main drainage system (right), or it may discharge to a soakaway (left). This will depend on local authority requirements

the existing hopper head illustrated on page 15. An upstairs WC in this case must be connected to a branch in the soil and vent pipe, and this will probably involve discarding the existing cast-iron soil pipes and replacing them with plastic pipes. A downstairs WC is best connected direct to the closest inspection chamber by means of a plastic branch drain.

With a single-stack system, which will probably be in plastic, connections will be fairly easy to make simply by adding extra branch inlets, as shown on page 16. Branch pipes should not be too long and should be at a shallow gradient.

At this stage, when you have studied not only the existing bathroom, but also the possibilities of exploiting other parts of the house, it is a good idea to marshall your thoughts by writing down what you intend to do. Make a note of whether you will be improving the existing bathroom or whether you are installing new fittings elsewhere. Make a list of all the fittings you want, and then study the list carefully in consultation with other members of the family to ensure that it not only meets current needs but will also be suitable for changing family circumstances in the foreseeable future. This could be the arrival of babies, the needs of children as they go into teens and adulthood, and perhaps the needs of elderly parents who may come to stay.

The list will help you not to forget anything when drawing up the final plans, and if you decide to have the job done professionally it will help you to brief your plumber or architect thoroughly so he will be better able to carry out your wishes.

Getting approval

Your preliminary list of proposals will also be invaluable when you come to discuss your plans with the local authority planning or building-control officer, because official approval will almost certainly be required. It is worth making an appointment to see the building control officer at a fairly early stage as

he will be able to tell you which parts of your project will need official approval.

Basically, changing an old fitting for a new one of the same type is classed as a repair, and official approval to carry out the work is not required.

However, if you alter the layout of the drainage, install additional fittings and intend to do something that will enlarge or alter the external appearance of the house, such as fitting an additional window or building an extension, then official permission will be required. This permission falls into two distinct parts: planning permission which falls under the provisions of the Town and Country Planning Acts, and Building Regulations approval.

Planning permission is always required if the house is a Listed Building, which means it has special historical or architectural interest or is in a conservation area. However, in the majority of cases planning permission will not be required because most average-size extensions will qualify as 'permitted development'. To be classed as permitted development, an extension must not enlarge a house by more than a fixed amount, nor exceed the height of the existing building, nor come further forward than the building line. The rules vary from time to time, so to find out if your proposals qualify as permitted developement or need planning permission, check with the local authority planning officer at the local town hall.

If planning permission is required, it will be necessary to submit plans in triplicate and pay a fee. Application forms available from the planning office will tell you what is required.

Regardless of whether planning permission is required, Building Regulations approval will be required for *all* building work – structural alterations, extensions, new and altered drainage, chimney work and the fitting of new heating appliances which are not a direct replacement of old ones.

In this case the person to contact is the local authority building-control officer, who will clarify whether your particular project will be classified as an improvement, in which case Building Regulation approval will be required, or a repair, in which case it will not. If necessary he will be able to supply application

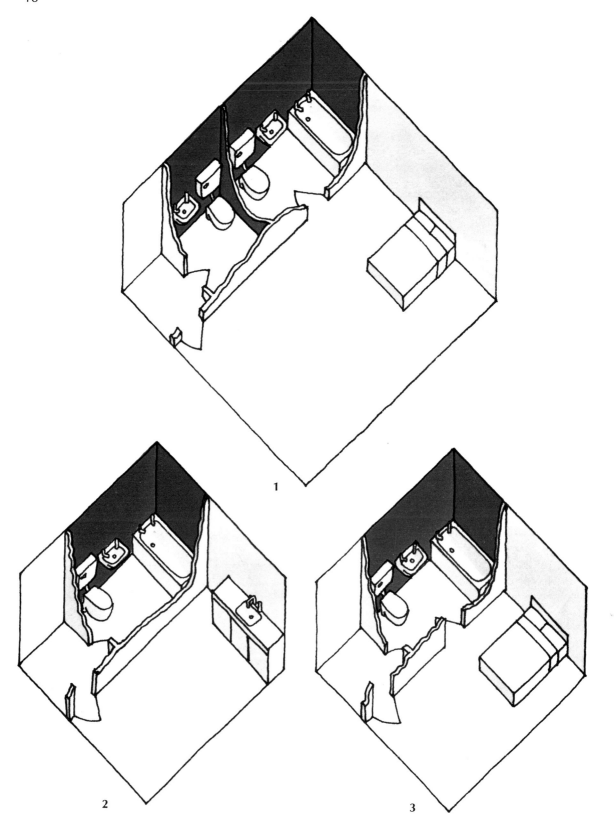

1

2

3

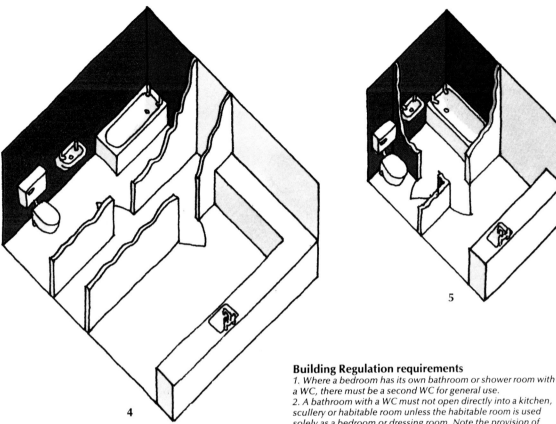

4

5

Building Regulation requirements
1. Where a bedroom has its own bathroom or shower room with a WC, there must be a second WC for general use.
2. A bathroom with a WC must not open directly into a kitchen, scullery or habitable room unless the habitable room is used solely as a bedroom or dressing room. Note the provision of circulation space outside the kitchen in this example, which satisfies the regulations.
3. If a bathroom opening off a bedroom has the only WC in the house, then it must have a second door so that it can be entered without passing through the bedroom.
4. Because this bathroom contains a WC, it opens on to a passage and not directly into the kitchen, and therefore complies with the regulations.
5. In this case the WC is in a separate compartment which opens into a bathroom and not directly into the kitchen. Therefore this arrangement also complies with the regulations

forms and he will be able to tell you how many sets of plans are required.

If your plans are reasonably modest and you take your time to draw them carefully, you should have no difficulty in applying for and obtaining the necessary permissions. However, if you have ambitious plans, or you just do not want to get involved with discussions with the local authority, then it is worth using a properly qualified designer, who may be an architect or a chartered surveyor, to draw up and submit the application. He will also commission builders and supervise the work on your behalf if you so wish.

Building regulations

As improvement work will have to comply with the current Building Regulations, it is worth looking at these at this early stage as they can

influence initial thoughts on planning. Apart from the Regulations concerning thermal insulation, which are continually up-rated as energy costs rise, the Regulations tend not to alter significantly. Obviously, though, before drawing up final plans do check that your proposals will comply with the current Regulations.

In fact, the Building Regulations are quite helpful with regard to bathrooms, cloakrooms and WCs. Whereas the regulations demand a minimum ceiling height of 2.3 m for habitable rooms (a room where you live, sit, eat, sleep or get dressed) this does not apply to bathrooms or WCs. While anything less than 2.3 m will probably be unsatisfactory, this concession could be very useful for squeezing washing or toilet facilities into a small space, such as under the stairs.

Also, it is not essential for a bathroom or WC to have an opening window and natural daylight. Instead it can have an extractor fan and duct connected to the outside air giving at least three air changes per hour. However, it must have one or the other and if it has an opening window or skylight this must be at least 1/20 of the floor area, and open directly to the outside air.

A separate WC, or a bathroom with a WC, must not open directly into a kitchen, scullery or habitable room, unless the habitable room is used solely as a bedroom or dressing room (see diagram on page 18).

If the bathroom opening off the bedroom contains the only WC in the house, it must have a second door so that it can be entered without passing through the bedroom, as shown on page 18. Alternatively, where a bedroom has its own bathroom or shower room with a WC, a second WC for general use must be provided (see page 18). Other examples of acceptable arrangements of WCs and bathrooms adjacent to habitable rooms are illustrated on page 19.

Raising money

It's all very well coming up with the plans for home improvements, but how do you pay for them? Well, for most people it will involve borrowing money, and the only consolation here is that the cost of borrowing will be reduced in most cases because home improvement loans to be spent on your main residence qualify for tax relief. There is a limit to the size of the loan which qualifies for relief, and this can be varied by the Chancellor of the Exchequer, but in the majority of cases the loan will qualify for relief. The institution where you get your loan will advise on the current qualifying limit, or you can consult your local tax office.

For the lucky few, the work may be paid for by a grant, and details of these are given below, but first let's look at the options for borrowing money.

The main sources for home improvement loans are *building societies, banks, finance companies* and *insurance companies*.

Before looking at any of these, you need to know exactly how much money you need to borrow. This involves working out the cost of materials, labour costs of any work you will sub-contract, professional fees, such as employing a chartered surveyor, and money for extras, such as a new floor-covering, wall tiles, paint and so on.

You need also to work out your disposable income, which is the surplus income after deducting your outgoings — mortgage repayments, rates, fuel bills, housekeeping and so on. Only by doing this can you be sure you will be able to pay off the loan you need. If you cannot afford it you can modify your plans at this stage before there has been any expenditure.

Fortunately, the Consumer Credit Act has made it easy for a borrower to see what the true rate of interest (the annual percentage rate, or APR) is on a loan, and what the total cost will be, before he takes out the loan. This makes it easy to work out whether you have got the disposable income to pay off the loan, and it also makes it easy to compare one offer with another. But do your homework very carefully before committing yourself to a loan.

Building Societies

The availability of money from building societies can vary according to how much money they can attract from investors. When money is scarce, borrowing for home improvements can be difficult because this form of lending is fairly low on their list of priorities, which is headed by finding loans for first-time home-buyers.

Preferential treatment is given to those with an existing mortgage, and to investors. Building society rates of interest are usually competitive, but the repayment period may be long. Although the size of the monthly repayments will be small, the total cost over the years will be high. Building societies are generally best for large loans over a long period.

Banks

Again, the availability of money for home improvement loans can vary, and the rate of interest charged will also vary with the status of the borrower. To obtain a loan will involve an interview with the bank manager who will want to know how the money will be spent and whether it is likely to increase the value of the property by an equal amount.

Banks are ideal if you want only a comparatively small loan, over just a few years.

Finance companies

Although the rates of interest may be higher than those charged by a building society or bank, finance houses are easy to deal with and can arrange an unsecured loan in less than a week after you have completed the fairly straightforward application form. Normally finance companies do not charge arrangement or legal fees, which is something you should check whenever applying for a loan from any source.

Insurance companies

An insurance broker will be able to offer free advice on loans through life assurance policies. Basically, policy-holder loans may be available to anyone with a life assurance policy that has a cash-in value, such as an endowment policy or a whole-life policy. The insurance company may lend between 85 and 100 per cent of the surrender value of the policy at a competitive rate of interest.

Local Authority grants

A grant is another source of finance that may pay for the improvement you have in mind. Basically, grants are intended for homes in urgent need of improvement and therefore you will be lucky (or unlucky, depending on which way you look at it) if your home qualifies.

The types of grant available and the amounts available vary from year to year so contact your local council for the latest details and an application form. Usually grants are dealt with by the home improvements officer or the environmental health officer.

At the time of writing there are four main types of grants, and being grants – not loans – it is well worth finding out about them before undertaking any work.

● *Intermediate grants* are for the installation of the basic facilities of an indoors WC and bathroom. These grants are a right provided a few basic conditions are met.

● *Improvement grants* are for carrying out general improvements in older houses to bring them up to a good overall standard. These grants are discretionary and it is for your local council to decide whether or not to give a grant.

● *Repair grants* also discretionary, are for pre-1919 houses needing substantial repairs.

● *Special grants* are available to the owners of houses in multiple occupation which need the basic amenities and a means of fire escape. Again, these grants are discretionary.

Layouts

With a general plan in mind it is time to sit down and consider the actual layout of the room, and here it is important to ensure that each fitting has enough space around it for it to be used comfortably and easily. Personal circumstances will also have to be taken into account because very often there is just not enough space available to give a fitting all the space you think it should have. However, you do want to be sure that there is sufficient space to stand in the bath and take a shower, for example, or stand beside the bath and towel yourself dry.

To help in this respect a lot of research work has been done on the optimum spaces that are required around the usual bathroom fittings, and as a result it is now generally agreed that the ideal user spaces are as follows:

Washbasin – needs a space of about 1000 mm wide by 700 mm deep in front.

Cloakroom basin – needs a floor space about 800 mm wide by 600 mm deep in front.

Bath – needs a floor space about 1100 mm long adjacent to the bath, and at the tap end if possible, by 700 mm deep. If the room has a sloping ceiling, position the bath so that there is at least 2200 mm headroom to allow standing room for drying and taking a shower.

Bidet – needs a floor space of about 800 mm wide by 600 mm deep in front plus space for knees and elbows at the sides.

WC – floor space 800 mm wide by 800 mm deep, plus minimum of 2000 mm headroom in front of the pan.

Shower – if enclosed on three sides needs a space 900 mm wide by 700 mm deep on the open side for towelling; if enclosed only on one or two sides needs a towelling space 900 mm wide by 400 mm deep.

Remember, these are optimum spaces and you may well be able to use fittings with less space. Also, these spaces can overlap if need be, which must invariably be the case in most small bathrooms. Remember, too, that although the majority of fittings are available in more or less standard sizes, the bathroom manufacturers do in fact make a large number of smaller fittings which may enable you to make the best use of all the available space. For example, while the standard bath is about 1700 mm long by 700 mm wide, baths as small as 1400 mm long by 800 mm wide, or 1500 mm long by 700 mm wide, are also available, both of which could be ideal in a small bathroom depending on whether you are short of space lengthwise or widthwise.

Conversely, if you have plenty of space it is possible to go for larger-than-normal fittings, and in this case baths approaching 1900 mm long by 1000 mm wide are available, and if you go to a corner bath these can measure about 1400 mm along each wall!

With these ideal user spaces in mind, detailed planning can go ahead. The actual positioning of the fittings in relation to each other will be influenced, as mentioned in the previous chapter, by the position of the door, windows and waste pipes, and to a certain extent the position of the hot and cold water supply pipes.

The first step, then, is to draw a plan of the bathroom on squared paper, marking on the plan the position of these features. Now cut out a piece of card to the same scale to represent each fitting and move these about on the plan until a suitable layout is achieved.

Some manufacturers of bathroom fittings produce useful planning guides for their fittings, consisting a squared grid on which the outline of the bathroom can be drawn. The guides also have outlines of a wide range of fittings to the same scale and these can be traced on to paper or card and cut out.

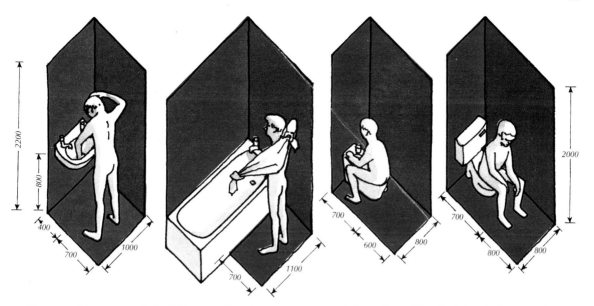

These are minimum spaces that will let you use the various fittings in comfort. More space would be advantageous. The space in front of a small handbasin in a cloakroom can be reduced to 800 mm wide by 600 mm deep

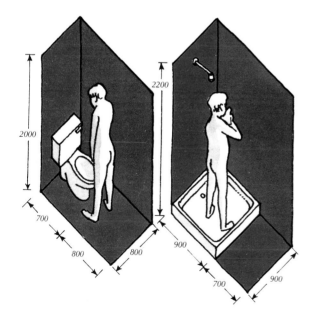

The towelling space shown for a shower is for one enclosed on three sides. Where the shower is enclosed only on two sides, the space can be reduced to 900 mm wide by 400 mm deep

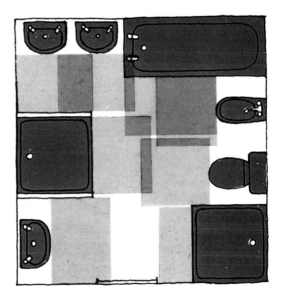

When producing a plan remember that the user spaces can overlap, as shown here in a bathroom which, for the purposes of illustration, is shown with three basins, a shower enclosed on three sides, and a shower enclosed on two sides.

Good layout ideas

With all the information that has been gathered from the previous pages on planning and positioning, you know all that is required on the theory of bathroom design to be able to produce your layout. But even so you may be still be short of ideas on good layout, so here, and on the next six pages, are some typical 'before' and 'after' situations which will show how various common layout problems have been overcome. You may not find a situation which is identical to your own, but there may be something similar, or you may see an idea ot two that you like and could work into your own plans for the new bathroom

It is common to have a WC en-suite in a bathroom as shown on the right. When the household is fairly large – mother and father, say, plus three or four children – this is not a very satisfactory arrangement, even when there may be another downstairs lavatory in the house. If the main adjoining bedroom is fairly large, with a dressing area for example at one end, it may be possible to extend the bathroom as shown below. The area taken from the main bedroom by building a plasterboard stud wall is balanced by building-in fitted wardrobes which help the room retain symmetry. Another plasterboard stud wall separates the new WC and there is a small wall-mounted hand washbasin. The bathroom is the same size as before (about 2440 mm by 1830 mm (8 ft by 6 ft) but now there is room for a bidet as well as a handbasin, and an overbath shower has been included

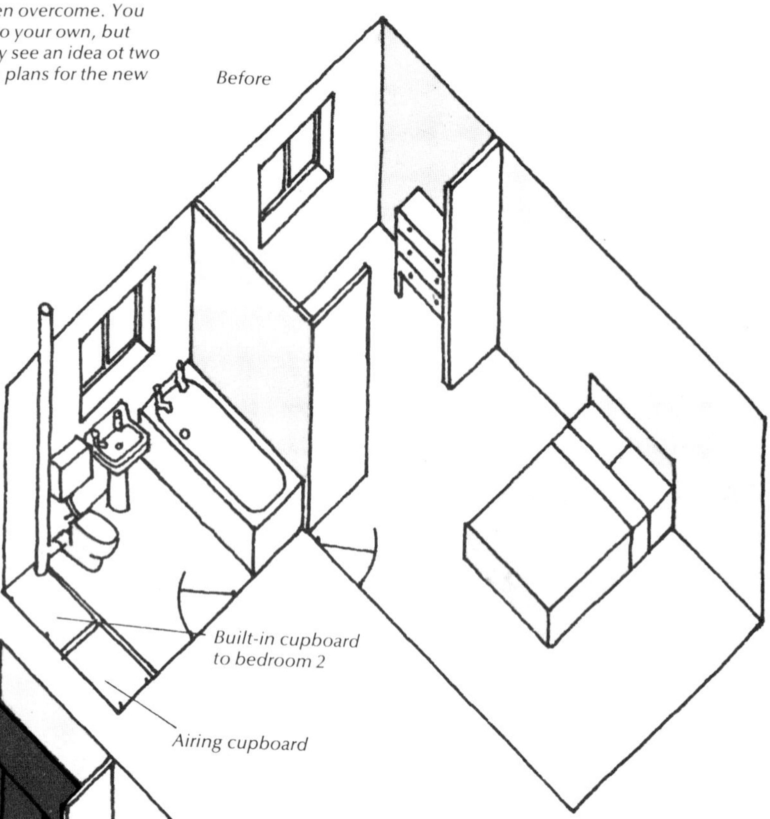

Before

Built-in cupboard to bedroom 2

Airing cupboard

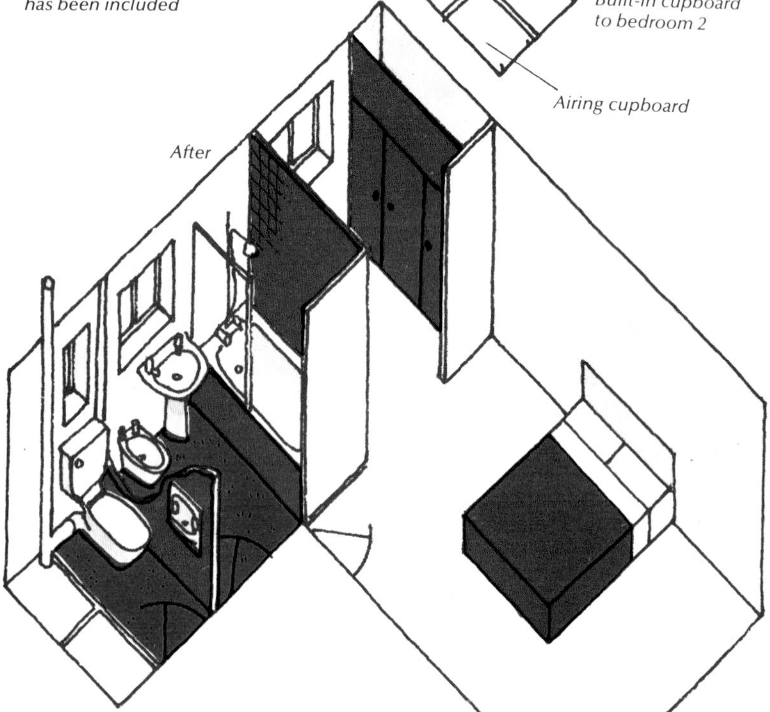

After

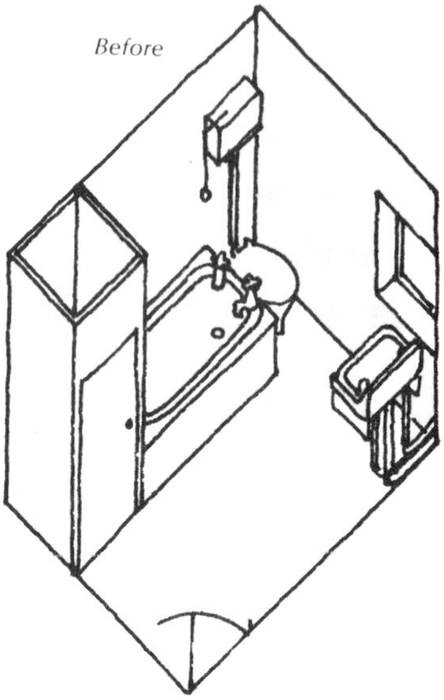

Before

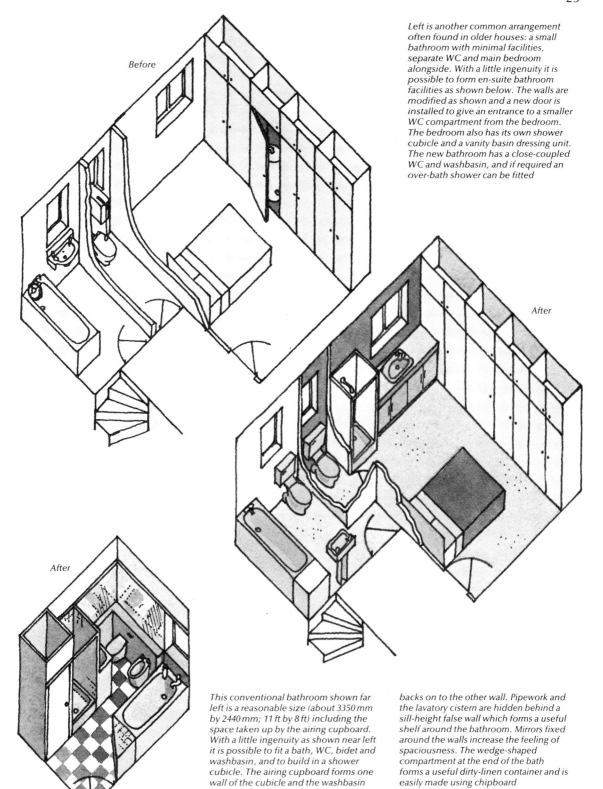

Before

After

After

Left is another common arrangement often found in older houses: a small bathroom with minimal facilities, separate WC and main bedroom alongside. With a little ingenuity it is possible to form en-suite bathroom facilities as shown below. The walls are modified as shown and a new door is installed to give an entrance to a smaller WC compartment from the bedroom. The bedroom also has its own shower cubicle and a vanity basin dressing unit. The new bathroom has a close-coupled WC and washbasin, and if required an over-bath shower can be fitted

This conventional bathroom shown far left is a reasonable size (about 3350 mm by 2440 mm; 11 ft by 8 ft) including the space taken up by the airing cupboard. With a little ingenuity as shown near left it is possible to fit a bath, WC, bidet and washbasin, and to build in a shower cubicle. The airing cupboard forms one wall of the cubicle and the washbasin backs on to the other wall. Pipework and the lavatory cistern are hidden behind a sill-height false wall which forms a useful shelf around the bathroom. Mirrors fixed around the walls increase the feeling of spaciousness. The wedge-shaped compartment at the end of the bath forms a useful dirty-linen container and is easily made using chipboard

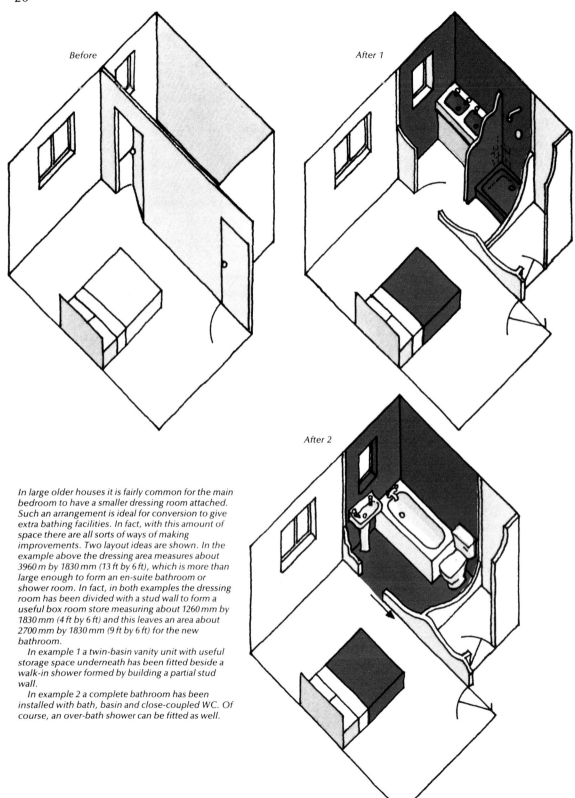

Before

After 1

After 2

In large older houses it is fairly common for the main bedroom to have a smaller dressing room attached. Such an arrangement is ideal for conversion to give extra bathing facilities. In fact, with this amount of space there are all sorts of ways of making improvements. Two layout ideas are shown. In the example above the dressing area measures about 3960 m by 1830 mm (13 ft by 6 ft), which is more than large enough to form an en-suite bathroom or shower room. In fact, in both examples the dressing room has been divided with a stud wall to form a useful box room store measuring about 1260 mm by 1830 mm (4 ft by 6 ft) and this leaves an area about 2700 mm by 1830 mm (9 ft by 6 ft) for the new bathroom.

In example 1 a twin-basin vanity unit with useful storage space underneath has been fitted beside a walk-in shower formed by building a partial stud wall.

In example 2 a complete bathroom has been installed with bath, basin and close-coupled WC. Of course, an over-bath shower can be fitted as well.

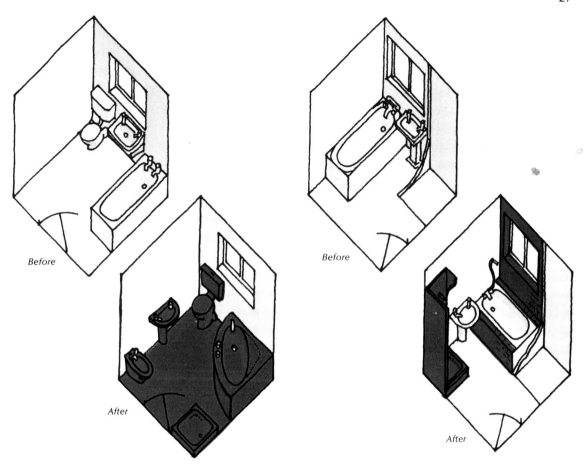

Before

After

Before

After

Often conventional bathrooms are the hardest to improve. Many late-1950s houses have bathrooms that are now showing their age, but at least such houses have rooms of a reasonable size which does give some scope for making dramatic improvements. A typical average-size bathroom for a house of this type is about 2600 mm by 2600 mm (8 ft 6 in by 8 ft 6 in). As the before and after views above show, it is quite easy to build a bathroom with all facilities into a room of this size. In fact, in the conversion shown it has even been able to incorporate a corner bath for an added touch of luxury. Such a bath needs a wall space measuring about 1400 mm by 1400 mm (4 ft 7 in by 4 ft 7 in) which leaves adequate space on one side for a shower enclosure measuring 770 mm (31 in) square and on the other wall to have a close-coupled WC suite. To the left of the entrance door there is space to fit a hand washbasin and bidet

Improvement work in this typical pre-war house is hampered by the siting of the airing cupboard in the corner of the 2440 mm by 2440 mm (8 ft by 8 ft) bathroom. Before conversion there was just a 1830 mm (6 ft) bath and a washbasin. It may have helped to move the airing cupboard, but often this is easier said than done. If the airing cupboard is not in the bathroom it will probably take up space on the landing, and moving it can mean drastic alterations to the heating and water-supply systems. The most practical and economic conversion is shown above. By selecting a slightly smaller bath measuring about 1520 mm (5 ft) long it is possible to re-site the bath so that it runs along the window wall, fitting into the space between the airing cupboard and end wall. A new hand washbasin is fitted on this wall and this still leaves room to fit a free-standing or built-in shower cubicle in the left-hand corner. A neat way to give the airing cupboard a facelift would be to fit a louvre door, for example

Before   After

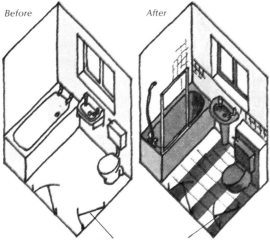

Door to airing cupboard

*In a small 'fifties' bathroom which has already got the major
facilities the scope for drastic alterations is limited. In this case,
improvements really boil down to smartening up the bathroom
by installing the latest bathroom fittings and wall tiles. In this
example the bathroom measures only 1700 mm by 1800 mm
(5 ft 7 in by 6 ft), and a further limiting factor is the door into the
airing cupboard. The conversion involves turning the modern-
style bath so that the taps are fitted away from the window wall,
which allows an over-bath shower and screen to be fitted
without causing problems of water splashing on to the window
sill. There is a pedestal basin, of course, and a close-coupled
WC. A practical point to watch here is that by using the existing
soil pipe in the floor this will have the effect of moving the new
WC pan and cistern forward and therefore boxing-in will be
required behind the WC cistern*

Before

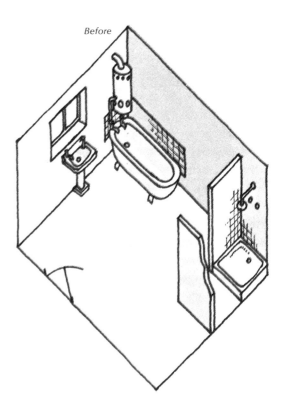

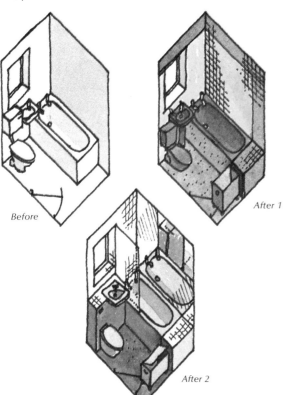

After 1

Before

After 2

*Often the bathrooms in old Victorian houses are really large
because they have been converted from old bedrooms. In such
cases the problem is mainly in using all the space effectively. In
the example above, the bathroom measures about 3660 mm by
4570 mm (12 ft by 15 ft) so there is scope to go to town with an
ambitious project. Two conversions are shown on the right.*

*In example 1 a peninsular unit has been formed with a slightly
raised bath and an arrangement of indoor plants which really
flourish in the warm, humid conditions of a bathroom. Other
facilities include a large shower cubicle with folding concertina-
screen doors, another cubicle with a vanity basin, and a third
cubicle with back-to-wall bidet and concealed cistern WC.*

*In example 2, part of the bathroom has been divided off with
a stud wall to form a separate WC area accessible from the
landing. This room also has a bidet and hand washbasin. The
bathroom itself has room for a shower cubicle behind the
entrance door and because a house of this type has high
ceilings it is possible to create a sunken-bath effect by building
a raised floor (as shown on page 63) with a wide step up to the
bath. There are vanity basins at each side of this raised area and
by carpeting the entire room it is possible to create a very
luxurious effect*

*Two more treatments are shown left for a small bathroom, this
time measuring 1500 mm by 2000 mm (5 ft by 6 ft 6 in). In
example 1 fittings have been up-dated and the space at the end
of the bath has been utilised by building a linen box on castors
which runs under the bath panelling.*

*In example 2 use has been made of a 700 mm deep vanity
unit/cabinet which houses a ceramic protruding front vanity
basin and allows a concealed cistern WC to be fitted. A
toughened safety-glass screen contains splashes from the
over-bath shower and a wall of mirrors gives an air of
spaciousness*

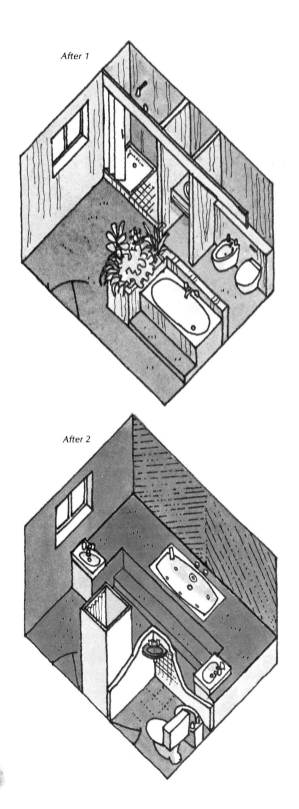

After 1

After 2

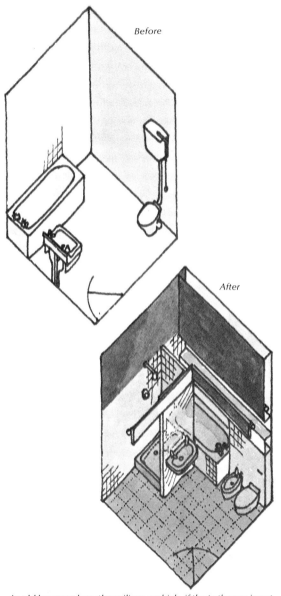

Before

After

In old houses where the ceilings are high, if the bathroom is not particularly large it can take on rather an empty box-like effect which is heightened by all the open space above head height. One solution would be to lower the ceiling by installing a suspended ceiling which may be boarded, or be an illuminated ceiling with translucent panels.

Another idea is shown above where the room measures 2750 mm by 2900 mm (9 ft by 9 ft 6 in) and the ceiling is presumed to be about 3050 mm (10 ft) high.

A dramatic effect has been achieved by grouping all the fittings at one side of the room with concealed lighting to heighten the interest. The bath is partially enclosed by a shower cubicle on one side and on the other side by the false wall on which a back-to-wall bidet and concealed-cistern WC are mounted. The washbasin is mounted on the shower-screen enclosure and in this way all the plumbing is grouped together.

The height of the room is effectively reduced by running a pine fascia board around the room at about 2150 mm (7 ft) high. This board conceals fluorescent lighting and the area above the board is painted in a dark colour to make the room seem lower.

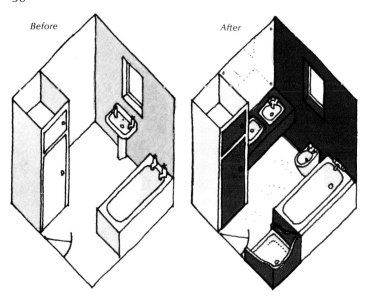

Before

After

Both the bathrooms on this page are fairly large, such as you may find in an old house. In this example, left, the bathroom measures about 2750 mm (9 ft) square and contains only a bath and washbasin. Even though the airing cupboard occupies space in one corner, there is scope for adding extra facilities.

One suggested layout would be to have a double vanity unit in a counter top on the airing cupboard wall, with a large mirror here to increase the feeling of space. The bath can be changed for a modern style and in the space between the end of the bath and the entrance door wall there is space for a shower cubicle. A bidet is shown beside the bath as this is easy to install, but as long as you were prepared to fit a plastic soil pipe this fitting could be changed for a WC if preferred

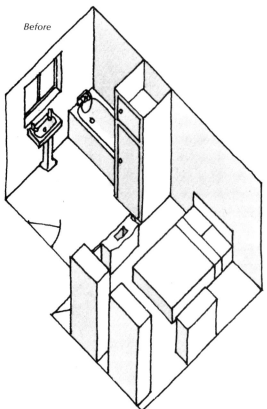

Before

After

When you have a fairly large bathroom adjacent to a main bedroom, it is a good idea to consider whether part of the bathroom could be sectioned-off and a new door formed so that the bedroom could have its own en-suite washing and showering facilities without reducing the amenities in the bathroom.

Such a scheme is shown above. The bathroom originally measured about 2750 mm (9 ft) square and had a linen cupboard in one corner which had to be moved so that a door could be knocked through the dividing wall between the bedroom and bathroom. To save space a sliding door is fitted here running up to a bricked-up fireplace which is left intact.

By building an L-shape stud partition wall for the new shower room it is possible to use the same wall to form another shower enclosure in the bathroom which also has a bidet. There is room for a shower tray and handbasin in the shower room

Fittings

If you want to be sure of getting a good-looking bathroom it is best to buy the fittings from one manufacturer. In this way you will ensure a matching style of the different fittings and also there should not be any colour variations between one fitting and another. This is not to say that you should never buy fittings from different manufacturers because it is common to buy, say, a cast-iron bath from one manufacturer, and ceramic fittings from another, but care does need to be taken to ensure that the designs are compatible and the shades match.

In general, bear the size of your bathroom in mind and choose fittings that are as large as possible, yet will still leave sufficient activity space around them to allow the fittings to be used in comfort.

Try also to anticipate future as well as present family needs when choosing fittings. For example, a fixed-outlet shower head may well suit a young couple, but when children arrive on the scene it will be much more convenient when showering them to have a shower head with a flexible hose connection. With a bath it could be a good idea to choose one with low sides, hand grips and a slip-resistant base in case an elderly relative takes up residence in the house.

Before looking at individual fittings and the points to look for when choosing them, it is well worth taking a look at the materials from which they are made and considering the advantages and disadvantages of each type.

Ceramics

Vitreous china and glazed fire clay are widely used for ceramic sanitary ware. Wash hand basins, WC suites and bidets are usually made from vitreous china. Fire clay is much thicker and heavier than vitreous china and is used for larger fittings, such as some shower trays and some larger one-piece vanity-unit tops.

Both vitreous china and glazed fire clay are hard and strong materials, with a fired glaze in many colours plus white. Both are smooth, easy to clean, and very resistant to abrasion and acids.

Ceramic fittings can be cracked or chipped if hard objects drop on to them so take care during installation to keep heavy tools well away from them. Vitreous china is non-porous, and even if the surface glaze is damaged it remains hygenic and germ-free.

Cast iron

Cast iron, which is widely used for baths and to a lesser extent for shower trays and vanity basins, is hard, rigid and very durable. Its finish of high-gloss coloured porcelain enamel is fused to the surface of the cast iron at 900°C to form a permanently bonded surface having similar properties to ceramic ware glazes. The enamelled coating is about three times as thick as on the average pressed steel bath. White and a wide range of colours are available.

Cast-iron fittings do not flex in use, and they are highly resistant to scratching and damage, and are very easy to keep clean. However, they are more expensive than equivalent steel or plastic types, and they are very much heavier. The weight can make a cast-iron bath difficult to lift into position during installation; certainly two men are needed to carry a cast-iron bath upstairs. It may also be necessary to strengthen the floor joists where a bath of this type is installed in an old, cottage-type property, or in a converted loft. In these cases take the advice of a chartered surveyor.

Designs tend to be somewhat plainer than found on plastic baths.

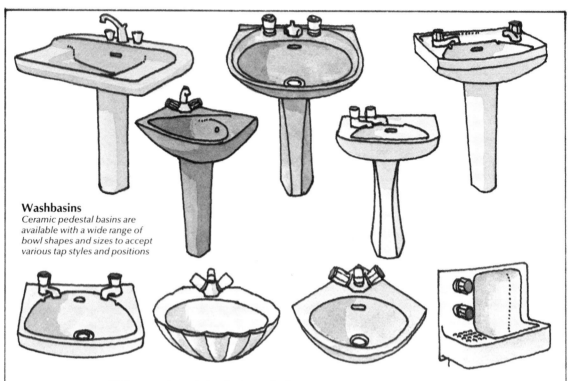

Washbasins

Ceramic pedestal basins are available with a wide range of bowl shapes and sizes to accept various tap styles and positions

Wall-mounted ceramic handbasins tend to be smaller than pedestal ones and are ideal for cloakrooms and bedrooms where space is limited. The semi-recessed type on the far right is particularly compact

Vanity basins

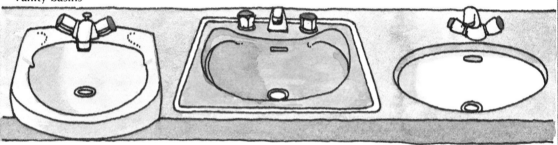

Partially inset, raised-lip ceramic countertop vanity basin with monoblock mixer tap

Pressed-steel countertop vanity basin with kidney-shaped bowl and three-hole mixer taps.

Fully recessed countertop vanity basin with monoblock mixer tap

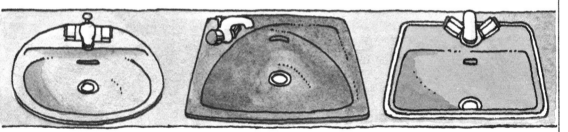

Inset, raised-lip ceramic countertop vanity basin with monoblock mixer tap

Distinctive offset design for a ceramic countertop vanity basin shown here with a monoblock mixer tap

Cast-iron inset countertop vanity basin with monoblock mixer tap

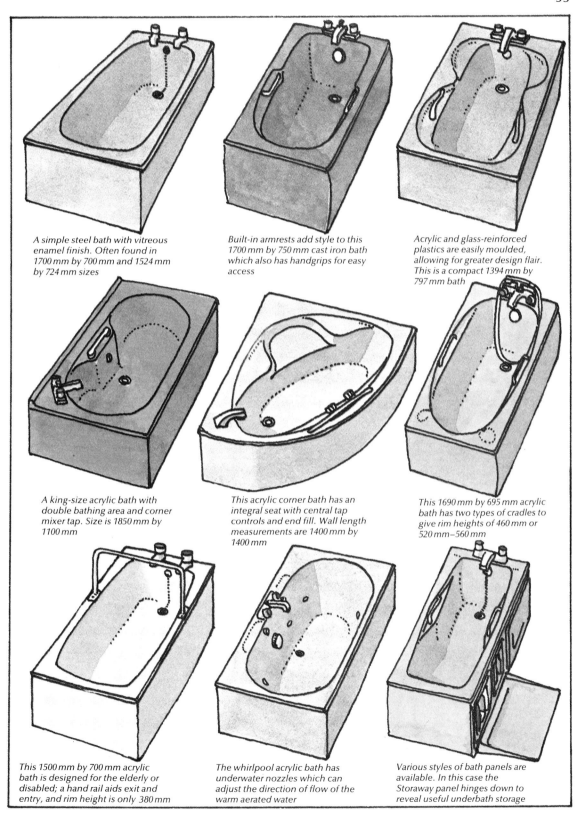

A simple steel bath with vitreous enamel finish. Often found in 1700 mm by 700 mm and 1524 mm by 724 mm sizes

Built-in armrests add style to this 1700 mm by 750 mm cast iron bath which also has handgrips for easy access

Acrylic and glass-reinforced plastics are easily moulded, allowing for greater design flair. This is a compact 1394 mm by 797 mm bath

A king-size acrylic bath with double bathing area and corner mixer tap. Size is 1850 mm by 1100 mm

This acrylic corner bath has an integral seat with central tap controls and end fill. Wall length measurements are 1400 mm by 1400 mm

This 1690 mm by 695 mm acrylic bath has two types of cradles to give rim heights of 460 mm or 520 mm–560 mm

This 1500 mm by 700 mm acrylic bath is designed for the elderly or disabled; a hand rail aids exit and entry, and rim height is only 380 mm

The whirlpool acrylic bath has underwater nozzles which can adjust the direction of flow of the warm aerated water

Various styles of bath panels are available. In this case the Storaway panel hinges down to reveal useful underbath storage

Pressed steel

Baths, vanity unit basins and shower trays made from mild steel are strong, but their rigidity depends on the thickness of the steel used. They cannot compare with the rigidity of cast iron, but they are more rigid than most plastics.

The usual finish is vitreous enamel, which is a fused-on pigmented glass and chemical finish with a high gloss that is resistant to scratching, acids and knocks. It is easy to clean.

Although pressed steel fittings are very resistant to breakage, as with ceramic ware, the glaze can be chipped if hard objects are dropped into them.

Plastics

Plastics are widely used for baths, WC cisterns, vanity-unit basins, and shower trays. Two types of plastics are commonly available; acrylic and glass-reinforced plastic (grp). Both are light in weight, and therefore easily handled during installation. They are warm to the touch which is useful for shower trays and when first getting into a bath. They are also resilient and resistant to chipping and because they are easily moulded they are available in a wide variety of shapes and styles. They are reasonably cheap and are available in a wide range of colours.

They have a smooth and glossy surface, but this needs to be carefully looked after because plastics can be easily scratched in use, particularly if cleaned with abrasives. They are also easily damaged by lighted cigarettes, and in a household fire they have been known to burn, giving off toxic fumes, although with luck this will be an unlikely occurrence!

Generally, plastics are harder to clean than the other materials covered in this section.

Because these plastics are flexible, large items such as baths and shower trays have moulded-in chipboard bases with rigid metal supporting cradles to stop the fittings from moving in use. Even so, the fittings will still need to be fixed to the floor and to the walls to prevent them from flexing.

Another type of plastic, polystyrene, which is not as hard as other plastics, is often used for ancillary items, such as bath and shower panels and bath-side storage units.

Choosing fittings

Washbasins

Basically there are two types; most washbasins are made from smooth, hard vitreous china in colours to match baths, and other fittings. Usually they are designed for mounting on a matching pedestal, but they can be wall-mounted. The other type is the vanity, or vanitory, basin which is designed to be built into a counter top or cupboard unit. The latter are excellent space savers and as such are frequently used as part of a storage system in bedrooms. Vanity basins are usually made from pressed steel, which is usually enamelled in the same way as steel baths, or they may be made from vitreous china, or various plastics, usually acrylic or glass-reinforced plastic (grp).

Pedestal washbasin units are useful because they allow the water supply pipes and the waste outlet to be hidden. In this case the height that the basin is fixed is decided by the manufacturer and this can be something of a compromise, being low enough for children to reach while not being too low for most adults. In a household of tall adults it may be more convenient to choose wall-hung basins which can be fixed at any height, but in this case remember to consider future family needs and the fact that lower basins may well be required when children come along. Wall-hung basins have another advantage in that they keep the floor area clear under the basin, but both water supply and waste pipes are visable, unless the basin is boxed-in or fitted on a false wall which can hide the plumbing.

Some basins are suitable for mounting on a pedestal or on a wall, but in general they are specifically intended either for wall- or pedestal-mounting. The pedestal types tend to be larger than the wall hung types, which can be as small as 355 mm wide by 255 mm deep for use in small cloakrooms or WCs. In fact, where space is really short there are semi-recessed space-saving basins and one such design has built-in mixer taps, soap tray and integral toilet-roll holder. Another possibility where space is short is to have a wall-hung corner basin.

Apart from these small basins for special purposes, usually it is best to go for a reasonably large basin which is not too shallow. Some designs are too saucer-shaped, which means that the water tends to slop over the front when they are used. Small basins also cause a lot of splashes to go on to the surrounding surfaces, and make tasks such as hair washing very difficult. There should also be a reasonably deep recess for soap because it is irritating to have a design that allows the soap to slip into the water. There should also be a fairly deep drain channel which will help to keep the soap dry.

Of course, washbasins are available in all the standard bathroom colours. Because the basin will be around for a fairly long time it could be an idea to choose a fairly neutral colour which would allow a wider choice of colour for the walls, floor and ceiling. An interesting recent development is the decorated washbasin in which a decorative motif border is incorporated into the glaze. Of course, the border is continued on matching fittings in the suite, such as the bath panel, shower tray, WC cistern and bidets.

Although vanity basins take up more space than ordinary washbasins they tend to make better use of the space by providing a useful storage area under the countertop while the cabinet is useful in that it hides the plumbing pipework. Because they are neat, vanity units are particularly useful for providing extra washing facilities in bedrooms.

There is also a recent trend to a wider use of vanity units in bathrooms to give a range of vanity units and fitted cupboards that will produce a fitted look in a bathroom after the style of a fitted kitchen. The flat-top surrounding vanity units is useful for storing cosmetics, and to relieve early-morning congestion of the washing facilities it is easy to set two bowls into the same countertop.

There are various styles of vanity units. The raised-lip styles are usually made from ceramic. A hole is cut in the countertop and the basin rests in it. The size of the hole is not critical in this case because the surround to the basin hides it, but as the basin is higher than the countertop, water that splashes on to the countertop cannot be cleared up as easily as it can into a fully recessed bowl. Some raised-lip vanity bowls are for setting entirely within the countertop, others are partially set into the top leaving the front edge exposed, and for very narrow cupboard units there is a vanity unit in which only the back half of the basin is set into the cupboard unit.

Another type of vanity unit, somewhat similar to the raised-lip types, is the complete ceramic-top unit in which the bowl and top is moulded in one piece to fit neatly over a cupboard unit.

Many vanity units, made from cast iron, pressed steel or plastic, have only a slightly raised metal trim edge, and again these are for setting in a hole cut in the countertop. The rim hides any inaccuracies when the hole is cut, and being only slightly proud of the countertop this does not make it too difficult to wipe up spilt water.

Yet another type of vanity-unit basin is for building under the countertop. In this case the hole must be cut very neatly because it is visible. The advantage is that water can be wiped straight into the bowl and the finished appearance is quite neat.

Countertops for vanity units can be made from chipboard finished with plastic laminate or ceramic tiles. In all cases the join between the vanity-unit basin and the countertop must be sealed with a bead of mastic or silicone rubber to prevent water penetration.

Baths

There is a surprisingly large range of sizes, shapes and styles to choose from, in cast iron, pressed steel or plastic. Whatever material you decide to choose, ideally the bath should be long enough to be comfortable, with a sloping end for reclining, and hand grips which will be especially useful if children and the elderly will be using the bath. The base should be reasonably flat to allow standing in the bath in safety and there should be a lightly-studded slip resistant area if the bath will be fitted with an over-bath shower.

The usual size for a bath is about 500 mm high by 1700 mm long by 700 mm wide which is quite acceptable for most needs. However,

WC pans

The two basic types of WC pans. Left: traditional washdown model with low-level cistern. This type is also available with close-coupled cisterns. Right: Double-trap siphonic model which will always have a close-coupled cistern

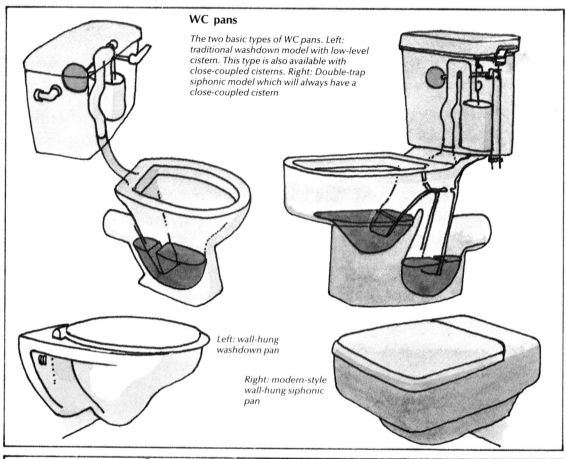

Left: wall-hung washdown pan

Right: modern-style wall-hung siphonic pan

Bidets

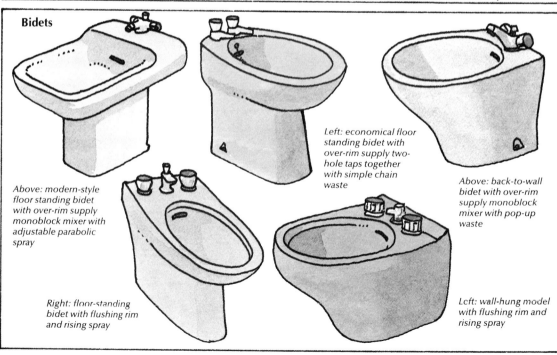

Above: modern-style floor standing bidet with over-rim supply monoblock mixer with adjustable parabolic spray

Left: economical floor standing bidet with over-rim supply two-hole taps together with simple chain waste

Above: back-to-wall bidet with over-rim supply monoblock mixer with pop-up waste

Right: floor-standing bidet with flushing rim and rising spray

Left: wall-hung model with flushing rim and rising spray

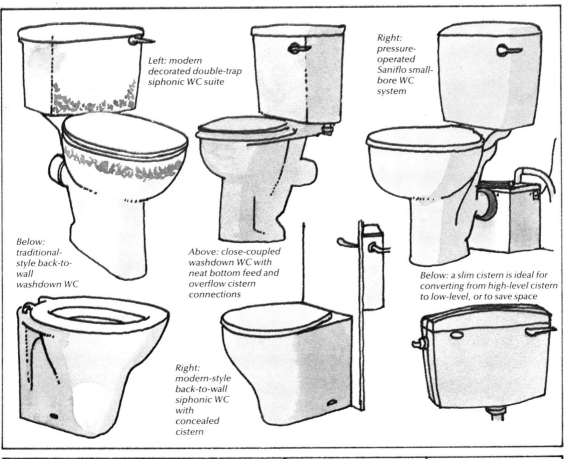

Left: modern decorated double-trap siphonic WC suite

Right: pressure-operated Saniflo small-bore WC system

Below: traditional-style back-to-wall washdown WC

Above: close-coupled washdown WC with neat bottom feed and overflow cistern connections

Below: a slim cistern is ideal for converting from high-level cistern to low-level, or to save space

Right: modern-style back-to-wall siphonic WC with concealed cistern

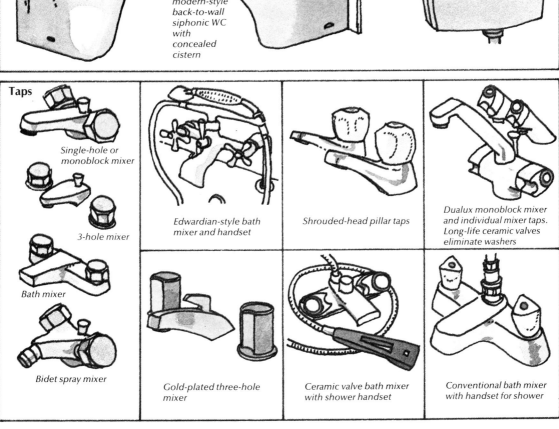

Taps

Single-hole or monoblock mixer

3-hole mixer

Bath mixer

Bidet spray mixer

Edwardian-style bath mixer and handset

Gold-plated three-hole mixer

Shrouded-head pillar taps

Ceramic valve bath mixer with shower handset

Dualux monoblock mixer and individual mixer taps. Long-life ceramic valves eliminate washers

Conventional bath mixer with handset for shower

kingsize baths up to about 1900 mm long by 1100 mm wide are also available. These vast baths can appear to be great fun, but on the practical side remember that they will take a great deal of hot water before you get a really useful depth of water for a good soak. Where there is plenty of room, corner baths are also available and these provide a measure of luxury at a reasonable price. Remember that with these larger baths it will be necessary to fit also a larger-capacity hot water cylinder.

At the other extreme, special short baths are available for use where space is restricted. These can be as little as about 1400 mm long, but tall people in particular will find they cannot use this type of bath comfortably, so try to avoid baths this small if at all possible.

When choosing a bath, apart from the features mentioned earlier look for built-in edges to hold soap and sponges. Also look at the bath panels which should match the style of the other fittings. These should be reasonably easy to fit and should be removable in case it is necessary to reach the waste trap at any time. Some moulded bath panels can be mounted either way up, which allows the styling of the panel to be varied slightly. Side and end panels should be designed for use in various combinations according to whether the bath is fitted in a corner, against a long wall, sandwiched between two end walls, or jutting out from a wall. However, do remember that you are not obliged to fit the proprietary panel, and there are various ways of making a bath panel to suit special purposes, as shown on page 95.

Another thing to examine is the position of the taps. Usually the holes for the taps and waste outlets are grouped at one end, but they are sometimes positioned at one corner, or in the case of the larger baths centrally on one side so they can be reached even if two people are using the bath. Cast iron and steel baths are always supplied with the tap holes ready-fitted, but some plastic baths can be supplied without tap holes so that these can be drilled exactly where required when the bath is installed.

A few specialised baths, such as the Oriental soaking tub, are designed for installation as sunken baths, but if this feature is required, most baths can be installed in this way. The most practical approach is to build-up the floor as shown on page 63, which is only feasible if the house has sufficiently high ceilings to give adequate headroom. Alternatively, if a suspended ceiling is fitted in the room below the bathroom it may be possible to achieve the sunken-bath effect partly by building-up the floor of the bathroom and partly by lowering the ceiling in the room below.

Whirlpool baths are another type gaining in popularity. In this case a mixture of warm bath water mixed with air is pumped at pressure through inlet nozzles fixed around the sides of the bath below normal water level. The nozzles can be swivelled to adjust the direction of flow, and water turbulence can also be adjusted by controlling the amount of air mixed with the water. These jets of warm aerated water provide hydrotherapy massage which is very relaxing.

The bath can be filled and used conventionally, of course, but by pulling a cord switch the whirlpool pump simply re-circulates the bath water. The pump and the pipework are all installed under the bath rim and there are only three water connections to make. The pump, of course, is earthed and is controlled on/off by a pull-cord switch for safety.

Bidets

These are made in vitreous china in white and colours, to match other fittings. As more and more people encounter them on the Continent, so they realise what useful fittings bidets are, not just for their accepted use, but as foot baths, for washing children and as a great help to the elderly and others who can only get into a bath with difficulty. Basically a bidet is a valuable adjunct to a washbasin; the washbasin being ideal for washing from the waist upwards and the bidet for cleaning from the waist downwards. And as long as the right type is chosen, a bidet is as easy to plumb in as a washbasin.

This easy-to-plumb and cheap-to-buy type is the standard bidet with over-rim supply: it works just like a low-level washbasin. It is also possible to get this type with mixer taps that incorporate an over-rim spray. In this case you sit on the bidet with knees facing the wall, so make sure there is adequate room around the bidet to allow it to be used in this way. A more luxurious type has a rim water supply in which the warm water warms the rim as it fills the bidet after the fashion of a WC pan. Again this type is quite straightforward to install and not too expensive to buy.

The type to avoid because it is both very expensive to buy and difficult to install is any bidet with an ascending spray in the base. The problem here is that the spray inlet is submerged and therefore there is a danger that dirty water can siphon back into the water supply pipes and pollute the water supply in the house. The water authorities therefore insist that this type of bidet has its own independent hot and cold water supply pipes and this makes the installation difficult. If you prefer this type, the manufacturer should be able to supply full installation details, although the main requirements are shown on page 94.

WCs

There are basically two types of WC or lavatory pan. The wash-down type is the most common and the cheapest. It relies on a downward force of water to clear the pan and this can make it noisy in action.

The other type is the siphonic WC, which although more expensive is the most efficient type and very quiet in action. The waste is literally sucked into the drains very efficiently while the flush of water cleans the sides of the bowl.

There used to be a wide choice of pan outlets to suit the soil-pipe (drain) position, but now virtually all pans are made with a short horizontal outlet which will suit any application. Using a suitable push-fit plastic drain connector this will give a 'P', 'S' or turned trap that will connect with the existing or proposed soil pipe.

Modern WC cisterns are invariably low-level, although the old-fashioned high cisterns are still available for direct replacement of an old cistern. However, it is more usual to replace a high-level cistern with a modern low-level type, and in this case special slim cisterns are available, which can be fitted without altering the WC pan position. Close-coupled cisterns, which are mounted directly on the back of the pan have become very popular because the flush pipe is not visible. In some cases the cistern is designed to be hidden behind a false wall, usually in conjunction with a back-to-wall or wall-hung pan.

Cisterns may be made from vitreous china, as pans, or from plastic. In the latter case make sure the colours are a good match. The same can be said for the cover and seat, which are invariably plastic. In the latest models these are an integral part of the design of the WC, and often they simply unclip for easy cleaning.

Ideally, every house will have at least two WCs, but one of the problems in installing extra lavatory facilities has been in the need to fit a suitable run of 100 mm diameter soil pipe to link with the existing soil pipe stack or drains. In many cases this is difficult if not impossible, as it would be in, say, a basement. The answer, however, could be to install a pressure-operated small-bore sanitary system. By connecting the WC pan into a shredder and pump unit, such as the Saniflo, small-bore discharge piping of approximately 22 mm diameter can feed into the soil stack instead of the traditional 100 mm pipe. The WC can be situated up to 20 m (60 ft) away from the soil pipe as long as the discharge pipe has a slight fall of 5 mm per metre (1/200). Alternatively, the shredder/pump will discharge the effluent 2 m vertically provided there is a positive fall immediately after the upward lift. The shredder and pump unit works automatically when the WC is flushed. The shredder blades rotate at nearly 3000 rpm, shredding the waste matter which is then picked up by the impellor pump and discharged through the outlet pipe to the drainage system.

Showers

Showers have become very popular fittings because they save space, time, and hot water. They can be fitted over a bath, or in a separate shower enclosure which can either be a factory-made pre-fabricated unit, or a purpose-built shower compartment.

For an over-bath shower the simplest arrangement is to have a push-on rubber-hose attachment which fits over the bath-tap outlets. These are really suitable only for hair washing and will contravene the water authority by-laws if the cold water supply is direct from the mains and not from a cold-water storage cistern.

A better arrangement is to have a bath and shower mixer. A lever on the unit will divert water from the taps to the shower spray. However, in this case it is still necessary to adjust the water temperature and spray force by carefully adjusting the hot and cold water taps. Again, the cold water supply must not be direct from the mains. Also, to obtain a satisfactory shower, there must be a satisfactory head of water – see page 93.

The best arrangement is to have a proper shower mixer which can be fixed to the wall over a bath, independent of the bath taps. The best mixers have independent control of temperature and pressure, allowing one to be adjusted without affecting the other. The best of all are thermostatically controlled mixers which maintain the selected water temperature and pressure virtually regardless of how much water is being drawn off elsewhere in the house.

With an over-bath shower some sort of enclosure is necessary to contain water splashes. The simpliest and cheapest arrangement is to have waterproof curtains hung from a rail. These must hang inside the bath. The folds of these curtains can be unpleasant to touch, and a more satisfactory (and expensive) arrangement is to have a folding safety glass or plastic screen or full enclosure mounted so that water flows back into the bath. An enclosure should be as large as possible so that the shower is easy to use, and the walls around the bath must be decorated so they are fully waterproof, which normally means tiling with ceramic tiles.

Without a doubt the ideal arrangement is a separate shower enclosure or compartment. In this case the tray and sides of the compartment should be as large as possible so that showering can be accomplished without rubbing against the side walls.

In a bathroom it is often comparatively easy to make a shower compartment using a separate shower tray, which may be cast iron, pressed steel, vitreous fire clay or moulded plastic. In this case the walls can be simple stud partitions

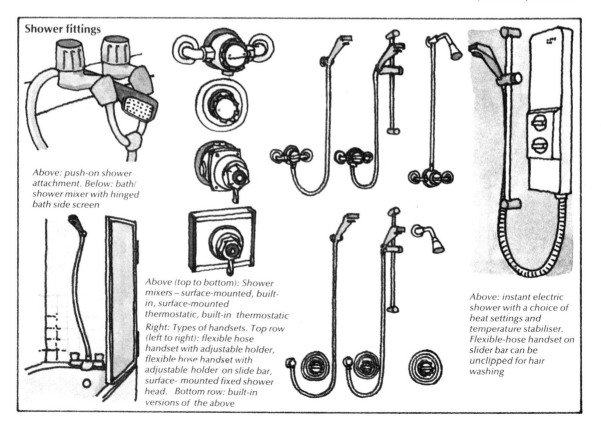

Shower fittings

Above: push-on shower attachment. Below: bath/ shower mixer with hinged bath side screen

Above (top to bottom): Shower mixers – surface-mounted, built-in, surface-mounted thermostatic, built-in thermostatic
Right: Types of handsets. Top row (left to right): flexible hose handset with adjustable holder, flexible hose handset with adjustable holder on slide bar, surface- mounted fixed shower head. Bottom row: built-in versions of the above

Above: instant electric shower with a choice of heat settings and temperature stabiliser. Flexible-hose handset on slider bar can be unclipped for hair washing

and the floor of an adjacent drying area made from water-resistant plywood or chipboard tiled throughout with ceramic tiles – see pages 54, 56 and 68. The shower can be provided from a shower mixer, ideally a thermostatically controlled one. If the compartment is made using stud partitions, it is usually a simple matter to hide the pipes in the wall, allowing a neat concealed mixer to be installed.

Shower enclosures are available separately, or complete with all the fittings. There are a wide range of types, with sliding, folding or hinged doors designed to be free-standing, built against a wall, built into a recess or built into a corner. These self-contained units are usually the best types for installing not only in the bathroom itself, but in bedrooms, on landings, under the stairs and so on. The sides can be toughened safety glass or plastic; check that they are properly sealed on to the tray. Where space is really short, a folding shower enclosure is available.

So far, all the shower arrangements mentioned have used the water supply from the existing cold and hot water tanks. but sometimes the system can be unsuitable for a shower. If there is not the minimum 1 m head of water – see page 93 – and it is not possible to raise the cold water cistern, then a shower booster pump should be fitted.

In homes where the water is heated by certain models of gas multi-point water heaters, it is possible to install a shower mixer as long as a pressure regulator is fitted into the cold water main to reduce the supply pressures. However, do check with the heater manufacturer or the manufacturer of the shower valve that the heater can be used with a shower.

If the multi-point is not suitable, and the cold water supply is direct from the mains, or even if it is just inconvenient to run the shower from the cold water storage tank and hot water cylinder, it is still possible to have a shower, but in this case it should be an instant electric type. Here, the shower heats the water as it passes through the heater, so the hotter you run the shower, the more the pressure drops. Instantaneous electric showers never give the forceful spray of hot

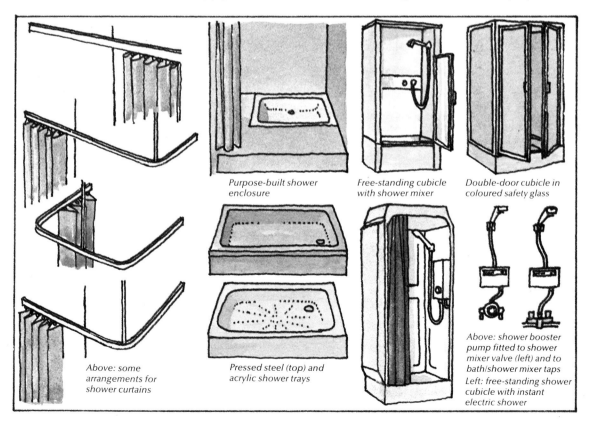

Purpose-built shower enclosure

Free-standing cubicle with shower mixer

Double-door cubicle in coloured safety glass

Above: some arrangements for shower curtains

Pressed steel (top) and acrylic shower trays

Above: shower booster pump fitted to shower mixer valve (left) and to bath/shower mixer taps
Left: free-standing shower cubicle with instant electric shower

water that can be obtained from a shower mixer. However, if you want to install a shower a long way from the hot water cylinder, say under the stairs, this could be the type to choose because it will require only a mains cold water feed.

Taps and mixers

There are many types of taps, most being chromium-plated cast brass. Gold-plated and gold-finish taps are also available, and becoming increasingly popular are taps with white or coloured stove epoxy finishes. Cheaper plastic taps are sometimes seen and these also have coloured or chrome-plate finishes.

Old-style taps have capstan heads, but modern taps almost exclusively have shrouded non-rising heads which may be metal, onyx or moulded plastic. In all cases the heads should be easy to turn, especially as children and the elderly are likely to use them.

Individual taps are usually pillar taps, in which the body of the tap is mounted in a hole on a flat surface, such as the rim of a basin or bath. Bib taps are occasionally seen in which the body of the tap is fixed to a wall and the supply comes from the back. Mixer taps have individual control heads, but the water mixes in the body of the tap and comes out of a single spout. Mixers can be made in one piece (monoblock), in which case the tap comes through a single hole in the fitting, or they can be made in three separate parts – two heads and a spout – interconnected with a concealed fitting, or the mixer may be designed so that body of the mixer and spout is mounted on the surface of the fitting. Many mixers incorporate a pop-up waste fitting which replaces the conventional chain and plug. Bath mixers often have a shower attachment, and it is also possible to get a bath mixer which has a neat retractable shower hose.

Styles of taps can range from the ultra-modern to copies of Victorian and Edwardian designs, and even older classical styles, such as gold-plated bird and fish spouts. Select the taps at the time of ordering the fittings to ensure that baths, basins and bidets are supplied with correctly spaced holes.

Water heaters

Most satisfactory is the conventional hot water cylinder heated by means of a gas, solid fuel or oil-fired boiler as part of the household heating system. Additionally, the hot water cylinder can have an electric immersion heater as a 'top-up'. The cylinder can also be heated by an electric immersion heater only, and in this case it should be on a white meter so it can heat the water using cheaper off-peak electricity. And, of course, it must be well-lagged.

Another system of hot water supply uses a gas multi-point water heater either in the bathroom or elsewhere in the house. This *must* be a balanced-flue type and it must be mounted on an outside wall so that the flue will connect directly with the outside air. These heaters are connected to the mains cold water supply and the water is heated as soon as a hot tap is opened causing water to flow through the heater. As these heaters draw their air from outside, they can be installed neatly in cupboards if necessary.

An alternative is the single-point instantaneous gas water heater which is the modern equivalent of the old geyser. One of these can be mounted above the basin or bath, or out of sight in a nearby cupboard. Again, it *must* be a balanced-flue type.

Electric instantaneous water heaters can only be single-point type. They do not have the output of the gas types and are suitable only for supplying hot water to, say, a hand basin or, as previously mentioned, to a shower. They can be handy when hot water is required in a remote part of the house, such as in a cloakroom, where to extend the main hot water system would create a wastefully long length of hot water pipe.

Where larger quantities of water are required by electric heating an open outlet storage water heater would be the type to choose. These heaters can be fitted over or under a washbasin or vanity unit, and are connected to the cold water mains supply. They vary in capacity, and when the cold water stored within them has been drawn off, there can be quite a long wait before the water has re-heated.

Decor and environment

While it is important to make a bathroom look warm, inviting and luxurious, it is essential not to lose sight of the fact that the room still has to be functional. Water is bound to be splashed about, the air will be full of condensation, and good ventilation should be balanced by adequate heating. Any decor materials chosen for walls, floors and ceilings must be able to withstand such conditions.

It is worth thinking first in general terms about colours for bathroom decor. Obviously, colour is a matter of personal taste and fashion, but it should be considered carefully because it does set the mood of the bathroom. And because many of the materials used for bathroom decor are quite permanent, like ceramic tiles, the colours should be chosen carefully. Likewise, texture should also be carefully considered. Colour and texture go hand in hand, and in the same way that colours should be chosen to harmonise with one another, textures should be chosen to contrast one with another. With bathrooms the tendency is to smooth and shiny finishes; the highly glazed surfaces of baths and other bathroom fittings, the finish of many ceramic wall tiles, mirrors, gloss-painted surfaces and the finish of many plastic laminates. All these will look at their best if there is a rougher texture to contrast with them (e.g. the pile of a bathroom carpet).

When choosing colours for bathroom fittings, remember the practical side of having to clean them after use. Lighter colours are generally much easier to keep clean and free from water marks than dark colours.

The safest colours to choose are the neutrals, such as beige, ivory and even white. They mix with most other colours and give an air of spaciousness. They have a subtle warmth with browns and wood grains or can give a striking effect with other stronger colours. On its own white has rather a cold and clinical effect.

Browns are warm, mellow, cosy and welcoming and have a restful back-to-nature appeal. The shades can vary from creamy brown to chocolate.

Yellows and orange-yellows are perhaps not as popular as they once were, but they are still warm sunny colours. They associate well with creams and browns and can be highlighted with a splash of green.

Blue tends to be cool, but clean. It looks good with white, as does red which used with moderation in a white bathroom will add a splash of warm, vibrant colour.

Pink has long been a popular bathroom colour; it's warm and feminine and goes with beige, grey and brown.

Green is a natural colour with a bright and clean appearance. Shades of green can be used together or with beige, buff, cream or white.

Walls

There is a wide choice in materials for bathroom walls, and an equally wide range of prices.

Assuming the walls to be plastered, as they will be in 99 per cent of all cases, the cheapest form of decoration is paint. You need a washable type, such as a good-quality vinyl emulsion which is available with a matt or satin finish. Gloss paint can be used, but this type tends to highlight imperfections in the wall, so check the plaster very carefully before using this type of paint. Gloss paint can also be more prone to problems with condensation on the surface than other types.

Where the plaster is not good enough for direct decoration, or where you want to give the walls a texture, they can first be papered with a relief wallcovering such as a Crown Anaglypta, Supaglypta or even a wood-chip, before they are painted.

If you are feeling adventurous you could paint a mural on a wall, but for most people to introduce a pattern will mean hanging a wallcovering. Any washable wallcovering is suitable, which includes washable wallpapers, vinyl wallcoverings and lightweight plastic papers, such as Novamura. Eminently suitable for bathroom walls are heavy-duty sculptured vinyls which are embossed to represent ceramic tiling. Incidentally, other materials for giving a ceramic-tile effect on walls are shiny plastic panels backed with expanded polystyrene. These can be quite effective if carefully fitted; they can be cut with scissors and fixed with expanded polystryene adhesive.

For textures on walls that are not likely to be splashed with water, several textured wallcoverings can be used. Vinyl imitations of hessians, silks and grass cloths are ideal. Genuine paper-backed grass cloths can be used, but fabric coverings such as hessian and silk are not suitable.

In almost all cases, all or part of the walls will be covered with ceramic tiles, which really are the only wall covering suitable for areas that will be splashed with water, such as beside baths and washbasins, and in shower areas. Even then, a waterproof tile adhesive should be used. Modern tiles are available in a wide range of colours and patterns, and all are easy to wipe clean.

Plastic laminates, such as Formica and Warerite, are available in a wide range of colours and patterns and are ideal for cladding bathroom surfaces as long as they are well fixed and the edges are carefully sealed.

There is also a wide range of decorative wallboards on plywood or hardboard backings which are suitable for bathrooms and cheaper than plastic laminates, although they are not so hardwearing.

Wood panelling is a popular and excellent wallcovering which, like decorative wallboards, can be useful in that it is fixed to a timber framework that will also conceal pipework and uneven walls. It can be fixed vertically, horizontally or at an oblique angle, but it must be thoroughly sealed with varnish to prevent moisture penetration.

Decorative cork in sheet or tile form gives an interesting texture which is warm to the touch, but this is not suitable for walls which are likely to be splashed.

A wall of mirrors or mirror tiles gives an easily-cleaned wall surface, but make sure the mirrors are good quality and suitable for bathroom use. The advantage of these is that they can appear to double the size of a small bathroom.

Windows

The advantages of double glazing are considered later. For the time being we will concentrate on window dressing.

If possible, curtains should be avoided. The vast majority of fabrics tend to absorb moisture when used in a bathroom and this tends to stain the curtains and make them sag so that they do not hang properly. The only exceptions are glass fibre, and perhaps Terylene nets.

It is far better to choose one of the many types of blinds that are ideal for bathrooms. Roller blinds are available in a wide range of patterns and textures, all of which can be wiped clean. Venetian blinds are also suitable and these have the advantage of having tilting slats which allow precise control over light admission. There are also many types of bamboo blinds which are suitable for bathrooms.

Walls and window decor
Walls: main drawing shows tongued and grooved timber panel cladding and ceramic tiles on main wall area. Note how the lower part of the wall surface has been built out to allow pipework to be boxed-in. Bathroom-quality mirrors on the wall beside the bath increase the feeling of spaciousness.

Windows: main drawing shows roller blind with scalloped edge trim. Inset panels: venetian blind (left); bamboo blind (right)
Alternative wall treatments in lower panels. Top row (left to right): brickwork-pattern relief wallcovering; sculptured vinyl wallcovering; tile-effect insulated plastic panels; plastic laminate; decorative wallboard
Bottom row: cork tiles; mirror tiles; stainless steel tiles; real brick slips; emulsion paint

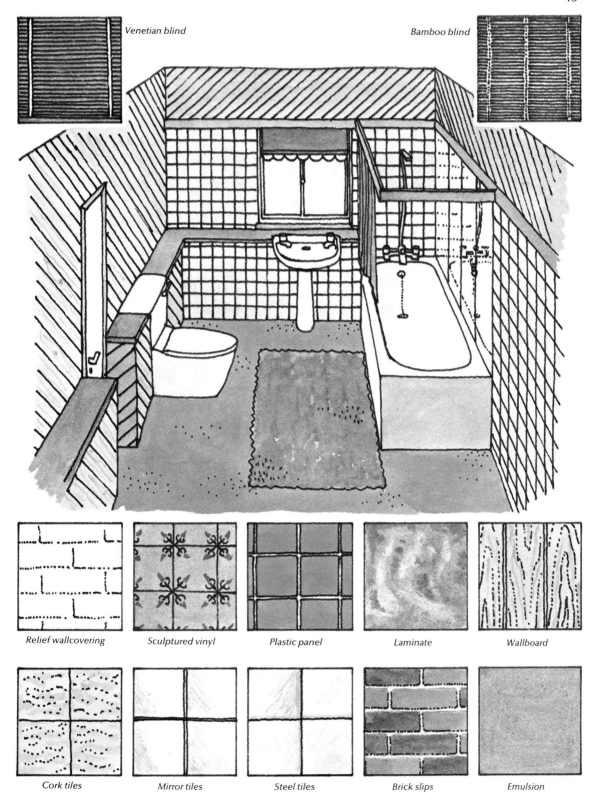

Venetian blind

Bamboo blind

Relief wallcovering

Sculptured vinyl

Plastic panel

Laminate

Wallboard

Cork tiles

Mirror tiles

Steel tiles

Brick slips

Emulsion

Heating

Adequate heating not only makes a bathroom a pleasant room to use, it also helps to minimise condensation by ensuring that there are few cold surfaces where condensation can form; while the air itself, being warm, can hold more water vapour than colder air. In most cases, because bathrooms are small, the cost of adequately heating them is not excessive.

The best form of heating is a hot water radiator or towel rail, or a warm air heating system which is part of an overall central heating system. Because bathroom heating is needed at times when the central heating system is turned off for summer, it is generally best if the bathroom radiator/towel rail is part of the hot water circuit, rather than on the main central-heating system.

As an alternative, or as an addition to this permanent primary or background heating, some form of independent heater may be required. Electric or gas heaters can be used, but they must be fixed in place. In the case of gas heaters they must be the balanced-flue type, and this means that they must be mounted on an outside wall so that the flue outlet/inlet has direct access to the open air.

Electricity and water can be lethal partners, so an electric heater must be connected to a fused connection unit and *not* simply plugged into a socket outlet. Electric heaters must be securely fixed to a wall or ceiling so that they are out of reach to anyone using the bath or shower. They should be operated by a cord-operated switch which can be inside the bathroom, or by a switched fused connection unit which must be outside the bathroom. For extra safety it is a good idea to have both types of switches so that in case of an accident the heating appliance can be switched off from outside the bathroom regardless of whether the door is locked.

Wall-mounted electric fan heaters are efficient at blowing warm air around the bathroom, except where ceilings are very high and thus warm air tends to accumulate above head height. A useful type is a warm air heater combined light unit that can be mounted over a mirror to keep the latter free from condensation.

Wall-mounted infra-red reflector-type heaters are efficient for heating small bathrooms while even neater are the ceiling-mounted combined infra-red heat and light units.

For gentle background heating, electric oil-filled towel rails or radiators are ideal. Again these must be fixed to the wall or floor and wired to a fused connection unit outside the bathroom.

Lighting

For safety, all light fittings should be totally enclosed and must have a shield or skirt to prevent anyone who is replacing a lamp from touching the metal lamp cap. Lights can only be controlled by a pullcord switch and the light fittings must be well out of reach of any shower spray.

A good general level of lighting is required. In a small bathroom one ceiling point may be sufficient, but in a larger bathroom it may be better to have a good overall spread of light using diffused fluorescent lights, a number of ceiling lights or downlighters, or by installing an illuminated ceiling. In addition, a light above a mirror will be essential. This should shine the light on to the face of the person using the mirror rather than down on to the mirror. If a small strip light is used, this should have a built-in switch and safety cut-out to isolate the lampholder when the tubular lamp is removed. If the strip light has a built-in shower socket, it should state that it is suitable for bathroom use (BS 3052). This means that it has an isolating transformer for safety and it will be a lot more expensive than the usual types which are not for bathroom use.

Electrics

Electricity has already been mentioned above under heating and lighting. In addition remember that it is highly dangerous and against the Wiring Regulations to install socket outlets (power points) in a bathroom, shower room or washroom. Never bring any electrical appliance (hairdryer, fan heater, portable television and so on) into a bathroom on a trailing lead after plugging it into a socket outlet outside the bathroom. The only socket outlet allowed in a bathroom is a purpose-made shaver unit fitted with an isolating transformer (BS 3052).

If the bathroom is fairly old, have the wiring checked carefully to ensure the cables are in good condition, properly earthed, and conforming to the current wiring regulations. Light fittings with flex pendants must be changed for ceiling-mounted types.

Ventilation

The cure for condensation is efficient heating combined with efficient ventilation. And good ventilation is also needed when the bathroom contains a WC.

Opening a window helps, but a better solution is to fit a spinning disc plastic window ventilator which allows accurate control of ventilation while cutting down on draughts. However, for really effective ventilation the only solution is an electrically-operated extractor fan. There are various types and sizes which can be window-mounted, wall-fitted, or even ducted (which is the only solution where the bathroom is away from an outside wall). The latter method is the quietest mechanical system and where it is the only method of ventilation the fan should be controlled by the light switch and a timer so that it runs for up to 20 minutes after the light switch has been switched off.

An extractor fan should give about 10 air changes per hour and the fan should have an efficient shuttering device to prevent draughts when the fan is not operating. Control should be by a pull-cord switch.

Lighting, heating and ventilation
Lighting: bathroom is shown with an overall illuminated suspended ceiling. A mirror-mounted light and fan heater unit heats the room and keeps the mirror free from condensation. A lazy-tong magnifying mirror helps shaving and make-up. The shaver socket is to BS 3052
Inset lighting on left (top to bottom): ceiling-mounted combined heat/light unit; circular fluorescent unit; strip light with built-in shaver socket to BS 3052
Heating: bathroom is shown with hot water radiator/towel rail. Inset (clockwise): electric towel rail: wall-mounted 3 kW fan heater: balanced-flue gas-fired wall heater
Ventilation: bathroom has louvre windows and wall-mounted extractor fan

Floors

A warm, non-slip surface which will tolerate the inevitable spills and splashes is essential. In fact, there is a good range of floor coverings that are suitable for bathrooms, and in the end the choice boils down to smooth or soft.

Top of the smooth floor coverings is vinyl sheet and there is a wide range of qualities, designs and colours from which to choose. Some types are hardly cushioned at all, but others are deeply cushioned with a foam backing and these are particularly comfortable to walk on in bare feet, and with their textured surface are more or less nonslip when wet. Vinyls are impervious to water and spills can be mopped up easily. Both 2 m and 4 m widths are available so even in a large bathroom there is no need to have joins. Go for a lay-flat type, which will not curl at the edges when laid and is highly resistant to tearing, making installation easier. The only drawback with vinyl is that it can be cold to walk on in bare feet unless the bathroom is adequately heated, but this goes for any of the smooth floor coverings. Rush and cotton bathroom mats can be used with vinyl to break up the somewhat cold and glassy appearance of vinyl sheet.

Vinyl tiles with self-adhesive backings are also suitable for bathrooms. They are easier to fit than sheet vinyl because they are in small, lightweight units, and a mistake in cutting means only one ruined tile rather than a whole sheet. However, there is a limited range of colours, and patterns in tiles, and although cushioned vinyl tiles are available, they do not approach the softness of cushioned sheet vinyls. There is also the potential danger of water reaching the sub-floor because of the many joins between the tiles.

This last remark also applies to cork tiles, which are attractive to look at and warm to walk on, but these too must be properly sealed to prevent moisture getting between the tiles and causing problems in the floor beneath.

Studded rubber floor tiles are becoming increasingly popular for bathroom floors because they are very safe to walk on even when wet, and are available in several colours as well as black. Water will not get through these tiles

to the sub-floor as long as the flooring is properly stuck down.

As long as ceramic floor tiles are properly laid (and they can be laid over timber floors) there is no danger of moisture penetrating this type of floor. Apart from being waterproof, ceramic tiles are also very hardwearing and available in a wide range of colours and patterns. Any ceramic floor tiles can also be used on walls to give a total coordinated look (but every wall tile cannot necessarily be used on a floor, so check the suitability for floor use when buying). The glaze on ceramic tiles can vary from a high gloss to a matt finish and the highly-glazed types can be slippery when wet. Ceramic tiles are very hard on the feet and they can be very cold unless the bathroom is adequately heated, ideally by underfloor heating.

For a soft floor covering a carpet is required and there are various types suitable as an overall covering or as mats in conjunction with one of the floor coverings previously mentioned. There is no doubt that carpeting is pleasant for bare feet and gives a bathroom a luxurious appearance, but it can be unhygienic around a WC and it can retain moisture. It is not therefore a good choice if it is likely to get wet frequently, which can limit its use when children use the bathroom. There are loose-lay synthetic carpets with rubber backs which are specifically made for bathroom use because they are highly absorbent and easily washed, but these tend to flatten in use. Carpet tiles are easy to lay and economical when it comes to fitting around baths. Most are loose-lay which means they can easily be lifted if it is necessary to dry them or replace any that are becoming worn.

Ceilings

In most cases a washable surface of good-quality emulsion paint will be suitable. If the plaster is not perfect, either line the ceiling with lining paper before painting it, or paint the surface with a textured compound which can be finished in various styles. If preferred, the ceiling can be papered as the walls, or expanded polystyrene or fibreboard tiles can be fixed to the ceiling with special adhesive.

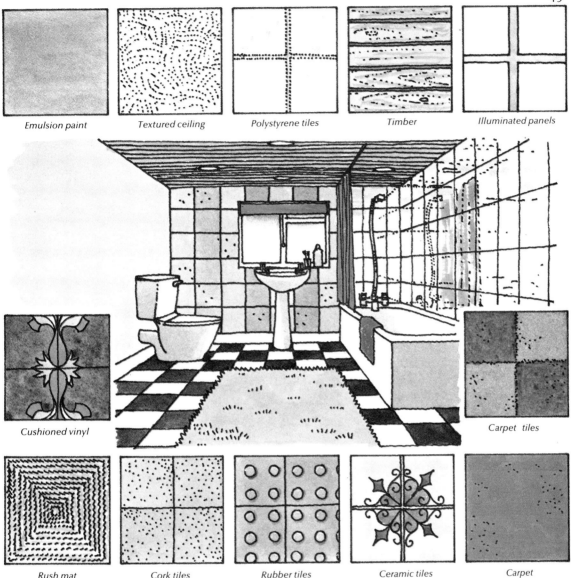

Emulsion paint   *Textured ceiling*   *Polystyrene tiles*   *Timber*   *Illuminated panels*

Cushioned vinyl   *Carpet tiles*

Rush mat   *Cork tiles*   *Rubber tiles*   *Ceramic tiles*   *Carpet*

To give a feeling of warmth the ceiling can be finished with timber cladding fixed directly to the joists or to a framework of battens. This gives an excellent opportunity to alter the lighting, perhaps by installing recessed down-lighters or spotlights. A ventilation duct could also be incorporated.

Another way to hide an ugly or damaged ceiling and disguise surface pipes, is to fix up a suspended ceiling. This can be used to lower the ceiling, which is sometimes necessary, for example, where the bathroom has been converted from a bedroom in an old house. A suspended ceiling can be made from timber and

Floor and ceiling decor
Floors: main drawing shows vinyl tile flooring with carpet mat. Panels around lower part of illustration show (anti-clockwise from left): cushioned vinyl sheet; rush mat; cork tiles; studded rubber tiles; ceramic tiles; bathroom carpet; carpet tiles
Ceilings: main drawing shows timber-clad suspended ceiling. Panels (left to right): emulsion paint; textured ceiling compound: expanded polystyrene tiles; timber cladding; illuminated panels

surfaced with plasterboard or timber cladding, or more easily made up from proprietary lightweight aluminium angles as a framework with infill panels of translucent plastic panels or fibreboard panels. In the former case, fluorescent tubes can be fitted above the ceiling to give an illuminated ceiling.

Practical work

Before getting down to the practicalities of making a new bathroom it is important to consider mould and condensation which are the two most common problems to be found in bathrooms. By understanding the cause of these troubles at the outset you will be able to ensure that all the improvements you carry out in the bathroom will minimise these problems.

Mould and condensation

In fact, mould and condensation go hand in hand, mould being the result of problems with condensation, or with structural dampness, so before going any further you should ascertain the cause of the dampness so that the appropriate remedial action can be taken. You may be able to spot structural dampness in the form of a definite leak or defect that allows water to penetrate the walls or ceiling during wet weather. On the other hand, if the damp patches get no worse in wet weather, and in fact tend to be worse in cold, dry spells, then condensation is the more likely culprit.

The acid test is to dry out the wall with a fan heater, then stick a patch of polythene sheeting or cooking foil to the affected area, sealing all round the edges with sticky tape. Leave the patch on the wall for a week or so and see what happens. If moisture forms on the outer surface of the plastic or foil, the problem is one of condensation; if it forms on the underside against the wall, structural dampness is the problem. In the latter case check the outside of the wall, looking for broken gutters and downpipes, cracked and missing rendering,

badly pointed brickwork and other external defects. If the problem is damp in the ceiling, make sure the roof covering is sound.

More than likely, though, the problem will be condensation. In a bathroom, large amounts of water vapour are generated and these are carried in the warm moist air until no more can be carried and then this vapour is deposited as water droplets on cold surfaces. The only way to reduce the problem is to strike a good balance between adequate heating and good ventilation, coupled with the insulation of cold surfaces, but in a bathroom you will probably never totally eradicate the problem because such forceful ventilation would be required that the room would be uncomfortable to use.

Choose a dry form of heating in a bathroom, such as electric heating or a panel radiator, and arrange good ventilation, ideally by having an electric extractor fan mounted high up and as close as possible to the main source of the steam, which will probably be the shower or bath. Wiring-up of an extractor fan is covered on page 77.

Effective insulation is the best means of minimising cold surfaces. Double-glaze windows, insulate both cold and hot water pipes before boxing them in, cover ceilings and walls with expanded polystyrene tiles or sheet linings under conventional wall coverings, or finish walls and ceilings with cork or timber cladding. WC cisterns in particular may suffer from condensation and in this case either box-in the cistern after packing around it with glass-fibre insulation, or drain and dry the inside of the cistern and then line it with slabs of expanded polystyrene fixed in place with epoxy resin adhesive.

Plan of action

If your bathroom update is to go smoothly it is important to have a plan of action so that the work can be tackled step-by-step in a methodical way so the chances of a mishap will be minimised. The actual sequence for completing the bathroom modernisation depends on whether the room houses the only lavatory in the house. This is the assumption in sequence 'A' below which ensures that the WC pan will be out of action for a couple of hours at the most, although the pan will have to be flushed with buckets of water between cutting off the water supply to the old cistern and reconnecting the new one.

Sequence 'B' indicates how the work can be carried out when there are alternative washing and toilet facilities in the house, which allow more time for building work and alterations to be carried out before the new fittings are installed. It is much easier to install fittings against previously built stud walls, for example, rather than try to carry out this type of building work around previously fixed bathroom fittings.

A. Bathroom and lavatory must be kept in use during modernisation

1. Buy bathroom fittings, pipes and plumbing fittings. Assemble tool kit (see page 10) and ancillary items, such as Plumber's mastic and PTFE tape, flux and solder (see page 80 and seq.).
2. Clean, then paper/paint ceiling, or install suspended ceiling (see pages 70–72).
3. Remove ceramic tiles/wallpaper/loose paint from walls.
4. Turn off water supplies to bathroom while retaining water supply to kitchen sink.
5. Remove washbasin.
6. Remove bath.
7. Remove WC cistern.

WC out of use
8. Remove WC pan (see page 52).
9. Make good floor (if necessary – see page 63).
10. Lay new floor covering (if possible, but *not* carpet – see page 64).
11. Fit new WC pan (see page 86).

12. Complete structural modifications, if necessary (see pages 55 and 63).
13. Fit new WC cistern (see pages 86–88).
14. Fit new bath/shower (see pages 90 and 92).
15. Fit new washbasin (see page 88).
16. Fit new bidet and/or separate shower.
17. Turn on water supply and check for leaks.
18. Apply sealant around bath/basin/shower tray *before* tiling (see page 95).
19. Box-in around bath/pipework/shower trays, etc. (see page 95).
20. Paint doors, windows, woodwork (see page 59).
21. Tile walls/floors (see pages 56 and 67).
22. Decorate walls (see pages 60 to 62).
23. Lay carpet, if required (see page 67).

B. Alternative washing and lavatory facilities available

1. As above.

WC out of use
2. Turn off water supplies to bathroom.
3. Remove old fittings – any order.
4. Remove old tiles/decorations from walls.
5. Clean, paper/paint or modify ceiling (see pages 70–72).
6. Carry out structural alterations/build stud walls, etc.
7. Make good the floor, if necessary (see page 63).
8. Lay new floorcovering (if possible, but *not* carpet – see page 64).
9. Fit new WC pan and cistern (see page 86).

10. to 19. As steps 14 to 23 in sequence 'A', above.

52

Water supply

It is most important that when the water supply is turned off to the bathroom there should still at least be a mains cold water supply at the kitchen sink so that drinking water can be drawn, kettles can be filled for hot water and buckets filled for flushing the WC pan until the new WC cistern is connected. If this cannot be achieved by shutting off the stopcocks or gate valves, it will be necessary to turn off the water supply for a short time while the hot and cold water supply pipes to the bathroom are cut at a convenient point and each one is temporarily fitted with a blanking plug, which will take only a couple of minutes using compression fittings (see page 9).

Clearing the decks

Washbasin

To remove this fitting, loosen the nuts on the tap connectors using a tap or basin spanner. If the nuts are tight, do not waste time trying to loosen then with penetrating oil or a blowtorch, but saw through the supply pipes using a hacksaw. It is easier to fit new pipes than try to save the old ones. The same goes for the waste pipe which will probably be difficult to undo, yet is easy to replace with a plastic pipe.

Bath

Cast-iron baths are extremely heavy, so get some help when removing one. Saw through supply and waste pipes. Either drag the bath out of place or break it up in situ using a heavy hammer, directing the blows to the curved part of the bath. In this case glass-like splinters of bath enamel will fly around, so wear goggles or safety spectacles as well as leather gloves and keep spectators well out of the way. The din can be terrific, so warn the neighbours what you are about to do before starting work.

If you want to save the wall tiles adjacent to the bath, adjust the feet so the bath is lowered before dragging it out.

WC cistern

Flush the cistern three or four times before turning off the water which ensures that the WC pan is as clean as possible. Use a spanner to disconnect the water supply pipe. If the overflow connection is tight, saw through the overflow pipe and replace it later with plastic pipe. Remove the screws holding the cistern to the wall and remove it together with the flush pipe which is simply pulled out of its entry into the back of the pan.

WC pan

On an upper floor the pan is likely to have a horizontal outlet. Remove the screws holding pan to the floor and then pull the pan forwards, rocking it from side to side as you do so. If the pan is cemented into the soil pipe, remove it as described for a ground floor pan, below.

On a ground floor it is likely that the pan will be cemented on to a solid floor and it will have a moulded-in S-trap outlet cemented into a stoneware soil pipe. This is now considered bad practice and modern pans are connected to the drains with plastic drain connectors.

To remove an old-style pan it will be necessary to break it. Remove the screws holding the pan to the floor and then drive a cold chisel under the front edge of the pan where it rests on the floor (near right). Ideally this will cause the outlet pipe to crack at the top of the bend above the point where the outlet runs into the soil pipe in the floor (middle). Sometimes gently tapping the outlet with a sharp bolster chisel will encourage the crack to form where you want it to. Avoid hitting the outlet directly with a hammer because this will send pieces of ceramic into the soil pipe and block it.

When the outlet has broken, lift the pan out of the way. Immediately tie a bundle of rags or newspapers to a length of string and push this into the soil pipe to stop unwanted smells and catch pieces of pipe which will fall into the drain when the collar is cleared away. This is done by tapping the pipe all round from the inside, breaking the pipe away in small pieces (far right). If a small sharp cold chisel is used, it should be possible to leave the soil pipe neatly level with the floor surface.

Before and after

In a small, cramped bathroom there is not a great deal of scope for introducing new facilities, apart perhaps from an over-bath shower, but contrast this small 'fifties' bathroom as it was with the colour photograph taken after the bathroom had been updated by the author. (The new suite is Armitage Shanks Wentworth with Marina bath and the tiles are Carmina by Langley London. Vinyl flooring is Nairn Cushionflor Sierra. Photographs by courtesy of Do it yourself Magazine)

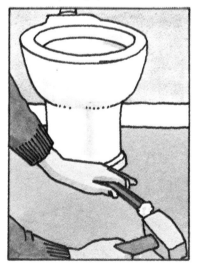

Wall repairs

Dampness

This must be cured before attempting other work. In a bathroom, condensation is likely to be a prime cause of dampness, so check for this as described on page 50. Once this has been eliminated, look to see if the trouble is caused by leaking water supply or waste pipes. These are probably going to be replaced in any case during the course of the job. If the walls become more damp during wet weather then suspect a structural fault, such as missing pointing (the mortar between bricks), exterior cracks, leaking gutters, and if the trouble is near ground level, a faulty damp-proof course.

Cracks

Fill with a cellulose filler if only small. With large cracks, check that the surrounding plaster is firm and remove it if it is loose. If possible, undercut the crack before filling it in stages with a gypsum plaster, such as Siraphite.

Holes

Treat small holes as 'cracks'. Larger holes should be chipped back to sound plaster and then filled to within about 3 mm of the surface with an undercoat plaster, such as Carlite Browning, followed by a surface coat of finishing plaster, such as Carlite Finish. The secret of getting a smooth surface is to wait until the finishing plaster is beginning to harden and then spray it lightly with water which will allow the surface to be polished with a flat steel trowel (called a float).

Loose ceramic tiles

Modern tile adhesives will fix ceramic tiles over well fixed old ceramic tiles. If a few of these are loose, remove them using a small cold chisel and then fill the hole level with the surrounding tiles using plaster filler. If many of the tiles are loose, remove the lot using a club hammer and sharp bolster chisel, or if necessary by hiring a small electric hammer (such as a Kango hammer) fitted with a combing attachment. This tool is especially effective for removing old-type ceramic tiles which were often bedded on a dab of mortar about 25 mm thick. When these tiles are left, there is always a problem in dealing with the top edge, especially where the bathroom was previously half-tiled and is now to be fully tiled (see overleaf).

Uneven wall surface

Walls must be smooth and sound if finished results are to be acceptable. In particular, ceramic tiles and mirrors must be fixed to flat walls. A bulge in one part of the wall may be caused by loose plaster. Chip this off and repair as for 'holes' – see above. If the whole wall is uneven it is best to dry-line it by covering the wall with a framework of 38 mm × 19 mm timber battens fixed 400 mm apart and packed out where necessary to give a flat surface. Then sheets of plasterboard should be nailed on to the battens and the joins between the sheets filled with joint filler and tape. As long as the plaster is sound the battens can be fixed over it using screws and wallplugs. However, if it is loose, then it is best to hack off all the plaster and fix the battens direct to the brickwork.

Door hanging

If a new door is being fitted in stud wall, a timber lining must be nailed to the sides and top of the frame which will neatly hide the vertical studs and protect the edges of the plasterboard lining. Simple battens nailed to the lining form door stops and an architrave moulding nailed around the opening hides the join between the lining and the plasterboard.

To hang a new door, first plane the edges to give about 3 mm clearance along all edges. Position hinges about 150 mm down from the top of the opening and 225 mm up from the bottom. Cut recesses for the hinges in the edge of the door and in the frame so that the hinge flaps are flush with the surface while the knuckle of the hinge (where the two flaps join) is clear of the edge of the door and frame. Hold the door on small wedges while the hinges are screwed in place. Test the fit of the door before fitting all the screws, then fit the lock and keeper plate on the frame.

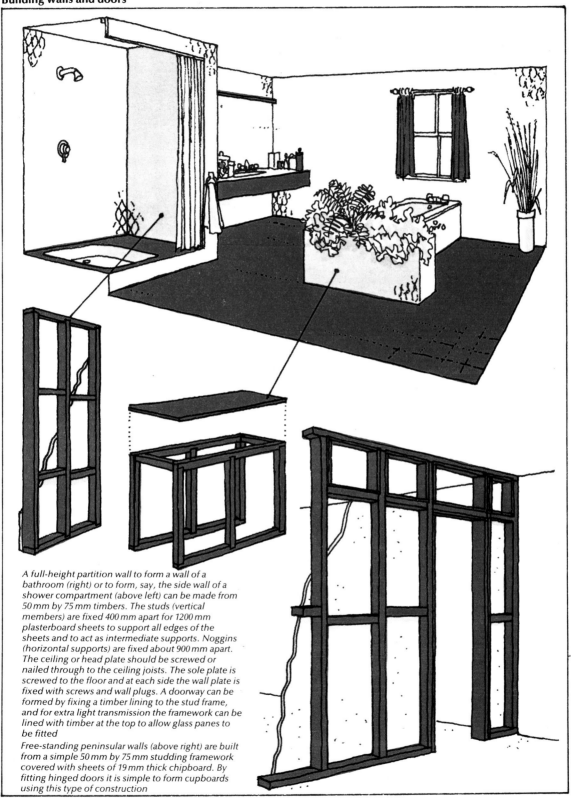

Building walls and doors

A full-height partition wall to form a wall of a
bathroom (right) or to form, say, the side wall of a
shower compartment (above left) can be made from
50 mm by 75 mm timbers. The studs (vertical
members) are fixed 400 mm apart for 1200 mm
plasterboard sheets to support all edges of the
sheets and to act as intermediate supports. Noggins
(horizontal supports) are fixed about 900 mm apart.
The ceiling or head plate should be screwed or
nailed through to the ceiling joists. The sole plate is
screwed to the floor and at each side the wall plate is
fixed with screws and wall plugs. A doorway can be
formed by fixing a timber lining to the stud frame,
and for extra light transmission the framework can be
lined with timber at the top to allow glass panes to
be fitted

Free-standing peninsular walls (above right) are built
from a simple 50 mm by 75 mm studding framework
covered with sheets of 19 mm thick chipboard. By
fitting hinged doors it is simple to form cupboards
using this type of construction

Ceramic wall tiling

Ceramic wall tiles are the ideal coverings for bathroom walls, but always fit them with a waterproof adhesive; the ready-mixed types are the most convenient to use.

Wall preparation

Remove wallpaper and loose paint. Sound gloss paint can be left, but rub the surface with coarse abrasive paper to provide a good key. If you are not sure whether the surface is sound, press sticky tape on to it and then pull it off and see if any of the surface sticks to the tape. If it does, the surface must be stripped off. Sound ceramic tiles can be tiled over – see 'Wall Repairs' on page 54. Alternatively, if care is taken the tiles can be fixed using a 'thick-bed' tile adhesive.

Planning

Whether the walls are being half-tiled, or tiled to the ceiling, aim to have a full tile in the top row, which will probably mean having cut tiles around the floor. Centralise the tiling on the wall so that there are equal-size cut tiles at each side of the wall and around windows. Make a measuring staff so that it is easy to work out where tiles will fall. The tiles are laid side by side (with plastic spacers between the tiles if they are the non-spacer type), and the staff is marked where the joins fall. If rectangular tiles are being used, another staff will be required for working out where tiles fall vertically. When tiling over a half-tiled wall, methods of finishing along the top of the old tiling are illustrated in diagram **9** opposite.

Setting out

The diagrams below and on facing page show a sequence for ceramic tiling. Use the vertical measuring staff to ascertain where the bottom row of full tiles will fall. At this point lightly nail a horizontal batten to the wall (**1**), positioned so that the top of the batten will support this row of full tiles. Use the horizontal measuring staff to ensure that this batten is positioned to support the tiles so that they are both horizontal and centralised on the wall. Now nail a vertical batten to the wall at one side of the room.

Diagram **1** shows how battens have been carefully placed to centralise tiling around a window. By careful planning, patterned tiles can be used to frame a window, Look at the view of the finished bathroom on page 53 and you will see how a pattern has been repeated on the other walls.

Fixing

Waterproof tile adhesive is spread on the wall to cover about 1 square metre and it is raked out using a spreader comb. Starting in the corner formed by the horizontal and vertical battens, the tiles are simply pressed into place (**2**). Continue to lay the tiles in pyramid fashion.

When the main areas are completed with whole tiles, the guide battens can be removed and the tiles around the perimeter of the walls, and around pipes, can be cut to fit. Good-quality tiles will cut easily if they are scored with a tile cutter (**3**), and then broken along the score line by placing in the jaws of the tile cutter and squeezing the handles (**4**). To cut curves score the cutting line as before and nibble out the waste with pincers. Alternatively, curves can be sawn out using a tungsten-carbide rod saw held in a hacksaw frame (**7**).

After the tiles have been in place for about 12 hours, use a rubber squeegee or damp sponge to work waterproof grouting into the joints (**8**). Wipe off the surplus grout. After 10 to 20 minutes draw a rounded small dowel along the joints to press the grout into place, and after a few hours the surface of the tiles can be polished with a dry duster.

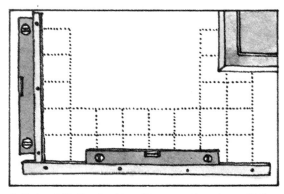

1. Horizontal batten fixed to wall to support lowest row of full tiles. Vertical batten at one side keeps tiling square. Note that tiling is planned to give equal cut tiles around window opening

2. After applying adhesive with spreader comb, tiling commences from one corner

3. To cut a tile, score along the surface with a tile-cutting tool that has a tungsten-carbide tip

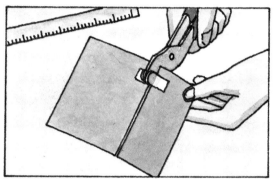

4. Snap the tile along the score line using a tile-cutting pincers

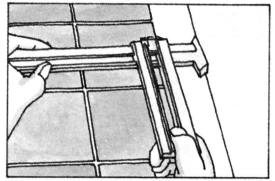

5. Some tile cutters have an adjustable marker for measuring gaps to be filled with cut tiles

6. Two score lines are made to cut a right angle and then the waste is nibbled out in small pieces using pincers.

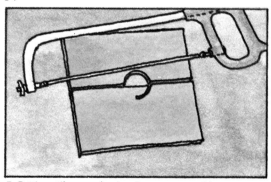

7. Cutting a tile around a pipe. Remove waste with a tungsten-carbide rod saw, or by using pincers

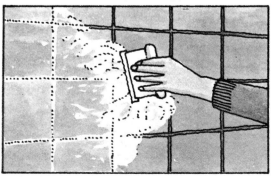

8. After tiles have been in place for 12 hours, apply grout to the joints. Wipe off surplus and polish tiles when dry

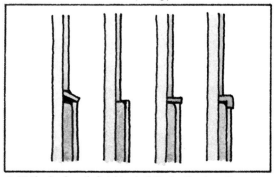

9. Methods of neatly finishing half-tiled walls when tiling over old tiles

Panelling walls

Fixing sheet panels

If the walls are perfectly smooth and sound, many sheet cladding materials, such as wood and plastic-veneered plywood panels, and painted hardboard panels like Laconite, can be fixed directly to the wall surface using a gap-filling panel adhesive.

The adhesive is supplied in a cartridge which fits in a mastic gun and it is applied to the back of the panel in a bead. The adhesive dries quickly so you must work fast, applying it near to the edges of the panel and in bands across the centre before pressing the panel in place and holding it still with wedges for a few minutes until the adhesive sets.

Being highly water-resistant, plastic laminate panels are ideal for bathroom walls, but as they tend to curl away from the wall it is best to bond them first to sheets of 19 mm thick moisture-resistant chipboard or plywood. These sheets can then be fixed to the walls with gap-filling panel adhesive or with screws and wallplugs, with snap-on screw covers to neatly hide the heads of the screws.

Where the wall surface is uneven or un-sound, line the wall with a framework of 38 mm × 19 mm battens fixed around the perimeter of the wall with vertical battens at 305 mm to 406 mm centres plus additional horizontal battens at 1220 mm centres. Fix the battens over a sheet of polythene which is held against the wall and acts as a vapour barrier. Thermal insulation can be fixed between the battens if required.

Screws and wallplugs will hold the battens, packing the underside where necessary with scraps of timber to produce a flat surface to which the panels can be fixed with contact adhesive or nails.

Before fixing the panels it is a good idea to seal the backs and edges of the panels with two coats of varnish. Seal all joints between panels, including the corner joints, with a flexible mastic, and then seal the surface of veneered panels with three coats of varnish, or two-part plastic lacquer, or a plastic coating.

Fixing timber cladding

Tongued and grooved timber boards can be fixed horizontally, vertically or diagonally. On a perfectly smooth and sound wall surface the boards can be fixed individually directly to the wall surface using a gap-filling panel adhesive. Usually, though, it is necessary first to screw a framework of timber battens to the wall surface over a polythene sheet which acts as a vapour barrier.

Again, 38 mm × 19 mm battens can be used, fixed around the edges of the wall and vertically across its surface at 450 mm intervals. There should also be horizontal battens at 600 mm spacings.

Fix the boards by secret nailing or clips and seal the surface with at least three coats of varnish.

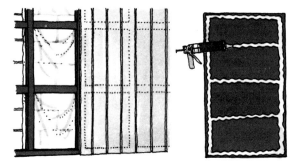

Walls: panelling
Various methods of fixing wall cladding. Left: tongued and grooved boards fixed vertically to wall battens screwed and plugged over a polythene vapour barrier. Right: panel adhesive being applied to the back of a sheet panel

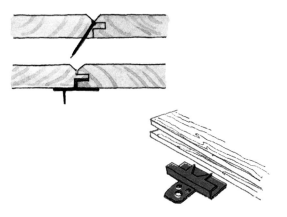

Top: tongued and grooved boards fixed by secret nailing. Above and right: the use of clips for tongued and grooved boards removes the risk of splitting boards when nailing

Painting – preparation

Surfaces to be painted *must* be sound, clean and dry.

Walls. Previously-painted walls should be washed down with sugar soap or weak detergent starting from the bottom and working upwards. Rinse with clean water and allow to dry. Gloss-painted surfaces should be rubbed down with wet or dry abrasive paper while still wet, after washing with detergent, but before rinsing off. This will produce a good key for the new paint to adhere to. Damp patches must be allowed to dry out once the cause of the dampness has been rectified. Dried stains should be coated with oil-based primer sealer. Flaking and powdery surfaces should be carefully scraped and sanded with abrasive paper wrapped around a block of wood. Seal with stabilising primer, or primer sealer. Fill holes and cracks with cellulose filler. Patches of mould growth should be sterilised by washing down with a proprietary fungicide or by using household bleach diluted in the ratio 1 part bleach to 15 parts water by volume. Leave for four hours and then treat again allowing 72 hours before redecorating. See also page 50.

Doors and windows. Wash, rub down and rinse as walls if paintwork is sound. Fill small chips with fine surface filler. Prime areas of bare wood. Peeling, pitted or chipped woodwork should be stripped using a blowtorch, hot-air stripper or chemical paint stripper (the only type to use near to glass). Prime the surface and then fill holes and cracks.

Doors (left): panelled doors – paint in order shown by numbers. Flush doors – paint in sections working from top corner to bottom. 1. Lay on paint with down strokes. 2. Fill in by cross brushing. 3. Lay off with vertical strokes
Windows (below): paint in the order shown by numbers

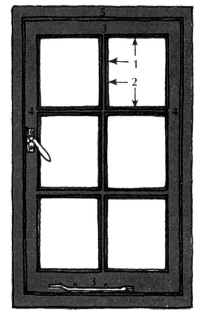

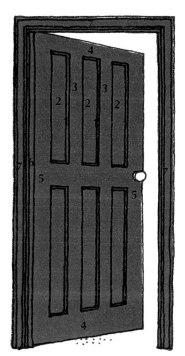
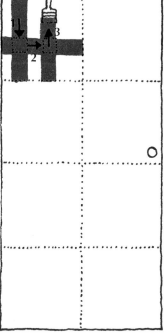
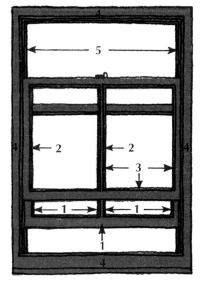

Painting – application

Walls. Work away from the window wall completing one wall at a time. Use a brush about 38 mm wide to apply a band of paint in the corners, just below the ceiling and around door and window frames. Cover the main area using a paint pad or paint roller in a random, criss-cross pattern working sideways and downwards from a top corner.

Windows. Use a cutting-in brush and allow the gloss coat *only* to slightly overlap the glass. Paint in the sequence shown in the diagrams on the previous page. Previously painted windows will need one or two coats of undercoat, followed by one coat of gloss. Stripped wood will need shellac knotting over knots, followed by one coat of wood primer, two coats of undercoat and one coat of gloss.

Doors. Follow the painting sequence shown in the diagrams on the previous page. Flush doors are painted in square sections working from the top left-hand corner to the bottom right-hand corner.

Papering

Preparation

Strip off the existing paper. Washable or emulsion-painted papers will have to be scored with a serrated scraper or piece of hacksaw blade to remove them. It may even be necessary to hire a steam wallpaper remover in some cases. If the wall is uneven or gloss-painted it is a good idea to first line it with lining paper hung horizontally. Loose, powdery or flaking material should be scraped off and the wall painted with stabilising solution before cross lining it as described above. Fill cracks and holes with cellulose filler and then size the walls with diluted paste and allow the size to dry.

Application

Start at the window wall and then work away from the window so that any overlapping joins do not cast shadows. Cut three or four pieces of wallcovering to length, matching the pattern in each case and allowing an extra 50 mm at top and bottom for trimming. Paste the paper generously and fold over the top edge to the centre line and then fold in the other half so that the pasted sides come together and the length can be easily handled. The paper must be hung vertically so draw a vertical line on the wall the width of the roll less 10 mm from the starting corner. The first length is positioned against this line and 10 mm of the paper will automatically turn the corner.

Smooth the paper on to the wall using a wallpaper brush, working the brush downwards from the centre to the edges to exclude air bubbles under the paper. Trim at top and bottom and wipe the surface with a damp cloth to remove excess paste. Subsequent lengths should be butt-jointed to the previously-hung pieces; try not to overlap joins. At internal corners trim the paper so that only 10 mm turns the corner. Measure the width of the offcut and mark a vertical line this distance from the corner. Hang the offcut to this line. There will be a slight break in the pattern where the offcut overlaps the previously-hung length, but this will not be readily noticeable. At external corners a full width of paper can be taken around the corner provided the corner is absolutely vertical. Probably it will not be, so in this case trim the paper so that 25 mm to 50 mm will turn the corner. Hang the length to the corner, but at this stage do not brush down the edge. Mark a plumb line on the return wall, hang the offcut and then brush down the loose edge of the first piece so it just overlaps the offcut and hides the join. Work quickly because the offcut will have to be moved up or down so that the pattern matches. In some cases the join will be less noticeable if the edge of the first piece is brushed down and then the offcut is hung to butt against the edge or to just slightly overlap it.

At windows, paper the sides and top of the reveal (recess) first, turning 10 mm of paper on to the surrounding wall. Fit two small triangular pieces into the corners at the top of the recess before papering the wall to the outline of the reveal.

Wallpapering

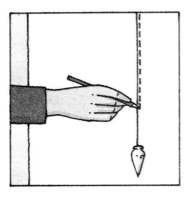

1. The first length of paper on any wall must be hung to a true vertical marked with a plumb bob and chalked string line or pencil

2. Hang the first length following the guide line; turn a 13 mm (½ in) margin on to the window wall and allow 50 mm (2 in) at the top and bottom for final trimming

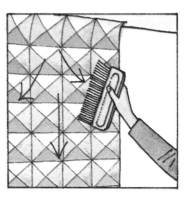

3. Make sure air is not trapped below the paper by brushing it down the centre and then outwards to the edges

4. Trim the paper at the top by creasing a line along the angle of the ceiling to wall using the back of the shears

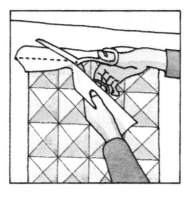

5. Peel the top back from the wall and trim carefully along the crease line

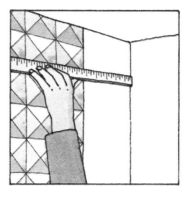

6. When approaching an internal corner, measure the distance to the corner at the top, middle and bottom. Add 13 mm (½ in) to the largest measurement then cut a strip to this width

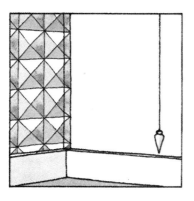

7. Suspend a plumb line as a guide to hanging the matching offcut of paper

8. At doorways, brush the paper on to leave it overlapping the frame. Trim off most of the excess

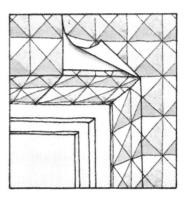

9. At window reveals, first paper the reveal turning 13 mm (½ in) on the facing wall, then cut the paper on the facing wall to the shape of the reveal

Other finishes for walls

In all cases make sure the wall surface is clean, dry and sound before starting work.

Cork

When in roll form, mark the wall vertically to guide each drop. Spread the adhesive recommended by the manufacturer over the wall area to be covered and rake it out with a notched comb. Hold the cork in a loose roll and working from the top of the wall, unroll the cork on to the wall, smoothing it into place from the centre outwards.

For cork wall tiles, mark out the wall as for ceramic tiles and tack a batten to the wall to support the bottom row of tiles. Spread cork tile adhesive on to the wall to cover about $1\,m^2$ at a time and then apply the tiles working out from one corner. When the main area is covered, cut and fit the tiles around the perimeter of the wall, marking them for cutting as shown on page 68.

Contoured vinyl

Deeply contoured vinyl is available in roll form to represent ceramic tiles, but it is hung and trimmed in a similar fashion to ordinary vinyl wallcoverings. The only difference is that a special heavy-duty adhesive is used.

Mirror tiles

Once again, mark out the wall as for ceramic tiles. It will help if a horizontal batten is tacked to the wall to support the bottom row of tiles. Mirror tiles are usually held in place with sticky tabs. Simply peel the release paper off the tabs before pressing the tiles into place. If it is necessary to cut tiles around the perimeter of the wall, this should be done by scoring the tiles with a glass cutter.

If the wall surface is undulating, the mirror tiles will highlight this so it may be necessary to line the wall surface first with plasterboard, chipboard or plywood.

Brick tiles

These are unlikely to be widely used in a bathroom, but they may be required for a special effect, say in an alcove. They are available in various colours and are fixed to the wall with a special adhesive which shows between the tiles to act as mortar joints. Sometimes a special pointing compound or even genuine mortar is used to fill the joints.

Plastic tiles

Plastic tiles in panels to represent ceramic tiles usually have a backing of expanded polystyrene, so in this case they are fixed to the wall with expanded polystyrene adhesive or ordinary ceramic tile adhesive. Plastic tiles are bendable and will cope with uneven walls. They can be cut with scissors and can even be bent around corners.

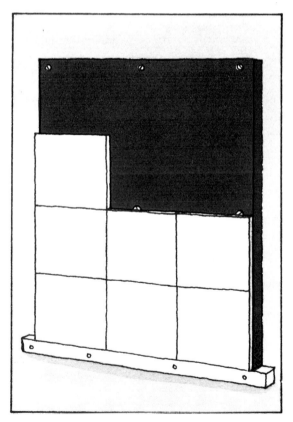

If the wall surface is not smooth, fix a plywood or chipboard-covered panel to the wall (right) and then fix the mirror tiles to this panel. Note the temporary batten of wood to support the tiles at the bottom while they are being fixed

Floors

For all types of flooring the sub-floor must be clean, dry, smooth and sound. If you suspect that the floor may be damp, then tape a piece of heavy gauge polythene on to the floor taking care to seal all round the edges. If water forms on the underside of the polythene after a few days then the floor must be damp-proofed. (Water on the upper surface is a sign of condensation – see page 50.) There are various brush-on membrane treatments which may be moisture-cured plastic sealers, or bitumen-based which when dry can be covered directly by the floor covering.

Uneven solid floors should be smoothed with a self-smoothing screed which is simply poured on to the floor, roughly smoothed out with a steel trowel and then left to smooth and harden. Cracks or larger holes should be filled with a general-purpose filler, or with quick-setting cement where speed is essential. Dusty concrete should be painted with a plastic sealer or a bonding agent to seal it.

Chipboard floors should be properly fixed down and large cracks between panels should be filled.

Timber floor boards must be well fixed and level. If uneven, punch down the nail heads and plane the high spots and fill the hollows before covering the entire floor with tempered hardboard. This should be fixed down with hardboard pins at 150 mm intervals. Fix the hardboard rough-side-up for most floorcoverings, except for self-adhesive plastic tiles in which case the hardboard should have the smooth surface uppermost.

Raised floors

Unless planned when the house is built, a true sunken bath is impossible to install without disrupting the room below the bathroom which will need a new lowered ceiling to hide the underside of the bath. A compromise is to build up a raised floor, perhaps with a step up to the bath. Of course an adequate ceiling height is required, but this should not be a problem in an older house.

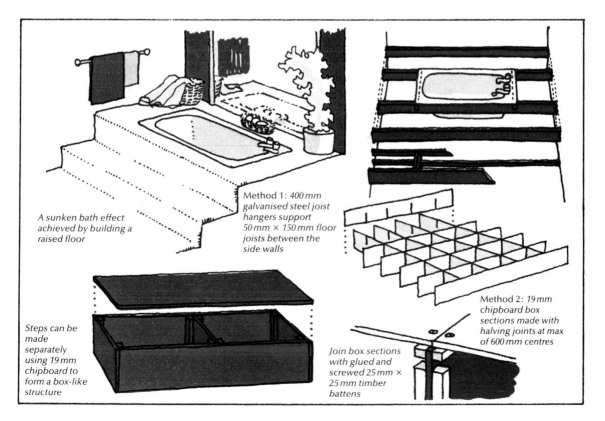

A sunken bath effect achieved by building a raised floor

Method 1: 400 mm galvanised steel joist hangers support 50 mm × 150 mm floor joists between the side walls

Steps can be made separately using 19 mm chipboard to form a box-like structure

Join box sections with glued and screwed 25 mm × 25 mm timber battens

Method 2: 19 mm chipboard box sections made with halving joints at max of 600 mm centres

Sheet floor coverings

Vinyl

Choose a good-quality lay-flat type in a width that will allow one piece to be laid without seams which are best avoided in a bathroom where quite a lot of water can get splashed about. The 2 m width rolls are the easiest to handle, but in a large room you will probably need the 4 m width. Sometimes 3 m vinyl is available.

In all cases, the task of fitting vinyl sheet will be made much easier if it can be done once the room has been stripped and before the new bathroom fittings have been installed. The vinyl will need only to be roughly trimmed around the perimeter of the wall as the wall tiles or skirtings can be fixed afterwards to come down over the roughly trimmed edges. Also, if the fittings like the WC pan, washbasin pedestal and bidet are screwed down over the vinyl there can be little risk of water penetrating to the floor boards.

Of course, it is not always practical to fit the vinyl first, and in this case in the average bathroom where space is limited and there are several obstructions on the floor, it will simplify fitting if a template is used to allow the vinyl to be roughly cut to shape before it is lifted into the room.

However, in all cases the first stage is to allow the vinyl to 'relax' before laying which involves leaving the vinyl loosely rolled, pattern-side inwards, for at least 24 hours in the bathroom, which should be as warm as possible to keep the vinyl supple. If there is not room even to stand the vinyl in the corner of the bathroom, then let it relax on the landing, or in a warm bedroom.

If the bathroom has been cleared, get the vinyl into the room so that the main part of the surface is smooth and the surplus vinyl is riding up the side walls. Make sure that the pattern lines up with the longest wall that will be seen when you enter the room, or with the bottom edge of the bath panel. It will make it much easier to fit the vinyl if the bathroom door is removed.

1. Allow vinyl to 'relax' by leaving it loosely rolled, pattern side inwards, for at least 24 hours in heated bathroom

2. After pulling vinyl into position check that pattern is centralised in the doorway and measure to a convenient line on the pattern to ensure it is aligned with the longest wall

If the template method is to be used, make the template from paper-felt or brown paper cut to fit as accurately as possible. It does not matter if you have to join bits of the template together with sticky tape, just so long as the result is a close-fitting template. Lay out the vinyl in a

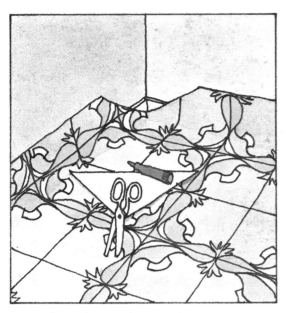

3. Trim off triangular pieces from internal corner positions until the vinyl is a perfect fit in the corner

4. At external corners make slanting cuts with a trimming knife until the vinyl can be pressed down to the floor

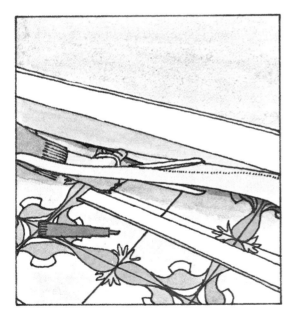

5. Check that the vinyl is smooth, then trim the edge around the room's perimeter. Fold back the vinyl so that a cutting line can be marked on the back and then trimmed with scissors. Err on the full side, then trim off slithers until the fit is perfect

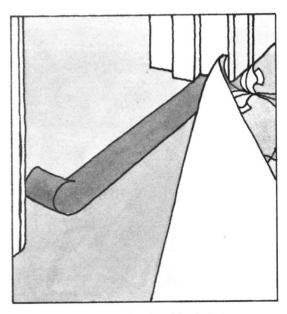

6. At doorways stick down the edge of the vinyl using double-sided adhesive tape

convenient place and position the template on top of it making sure that the pattern is centred in the door opening or against the longest wall. Cut the vinyl about 50 mm oversize all round and then take it into the room and lay it down so it is as flat as possible. Release cuts, which should not be seen from the front, will have to be made behind pedestal fittings and the WC pan to allow the vinyl to be laid round these.

Fit the internal corners next by folding the vinyl so the approximate corner position can be marked on the back, and then trim off a triangle

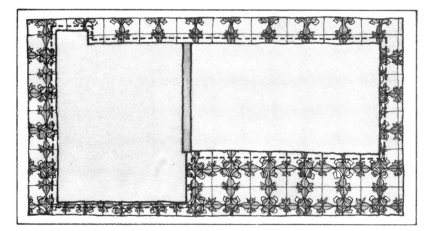

7. If bathroom fittings are already in place it is best to use the template method to cut the vinyl sheet roughly to shape. Make the template from felt paper, brown paper or even newspapers. It doesn't matter if you have to stick several sheets together. Lay the vinyl out on a flat surface, such as the lawn, get the pattern neatly lined up, and then cut the vinyl about 50 mm oversize all round

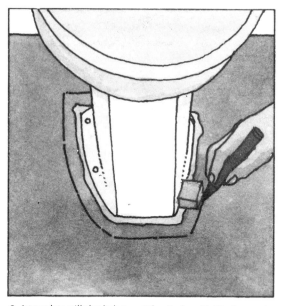

8. A template will also help to get the vinyl neatly fitted around pedestals. First position the template accurately in the room, and then very roughly tear it to shape around the pedestal. Take a small block of wood and while holding the block against the pedestal, mark all round on the template using a pencil

9. Move the template on the vinyl, and with it accurately positioned so that the vinyl will fit into the corners of the room, use the same block of wood to transfer the mark back from the template on to the vinyl. Trim vinyl to the line, and with a release cut made back to the wall behind the pedestal, the vinyl should fit perfectly when it is positioned

little by little until the vinyl is a perfect fit. At external corners, around door frames, and around the base of bathroom fittings, a number of downward-slanting release cuts will have to be made until the vinyl can be pressed down to the floor. By this stage the vinyl should be perfectly smooth.

It remains only to trim off the surplus vinyl round the base of the fittings. Because lay-flat vinyl is very flexible, the easiest way to do this to get a smooth edge is to fold back the edge of the vinyl so that a series of dots can be marked on the back of the vinyl along the cutting line. Pull back the vinyl so it lays flat and join up the dots with a rule and then cut along this line with scissors. Test the fit of the vinyl as you proceed, and if necessary trim slithers off the edge until the fit is perfect. The same technique can be used around the base of the bathroom fittings.

Lay-flat vinyl needs only to be stuck down at doorways, which can be done with double-sided sticky tape. If preferred an aluminium threshold bar can be used to hold down the vinyl at a doorway.

Carpet

Fitting bathroom carpet is very similar to fitting vinyl. It has a rubber back and can be cut with scissors. It should not be fixed down so that it can be lifted for washing and drying. For an even more luxurious feeling, this type of carpet can be laid on a conventional rubber underlay if required. To minimise the danger of water getting under the carpet and soaking the floor it is a good idea to ensure that there is some sort of impervious floorcovering, such as vinyl tiles, under the carpet.

Tile floor coverings

Cork, vinyl and ceramic tiles are the types most commonly used. In each case the floor preparation (see page 63) and the setting-out procedure is the same. However, ceramic floor tiles need a particularly stable sub-floor. A solid floor is ideal, but ceramic tiles can be laid on a timber floor as long as the surface is covered with sheets of 9.5 mm thick plywood, or tongued and grooved flooring-grade chipboard fixed down to the floor with zinc-plated countersunk-head chipboard screws at 300 mm centres. To improve adhesion in this case, the floor surface should be brushed over with a PVA bonding agent which is allowed to dry before the tile adhesive is spread.

Setting out

Tiled floors look best when laid from the centre, with equal width cut tiles around the perimeter of the floor. To find the centre point of the room, attach a length of chalked string to nails driven in at the mid-points of opposite walls. Draw the string tight and then snap it against the floor to make a mark. Repeat the operation on the adjacent walls so that the room is divided into four equal segments.

Now lay a trial row of tiles, without adhesive, along the chalk lines in a row from the centre point. If the last tile is less than half a tile in width, move the string line half a tile width off

centre and remark the line. If the layout leaves small pieces of tiles at doorways, you may have to put up with having narrow tiles against one wall if this avoids having narrow tiles in the doorway where they will be noticed. It is also important to check that the string lines bisect each other exactly at right angles. The best way to do this is to measure 300 mm along one line, 400 mm along another, and check that these points are 500 mm apart.

Laying tiles (see illustrations overleaf)

Work from the centre point, laying the first row of tiles accurately on the chalk line. Build out pyramid fashion from the centre until all the whole tiles are laid leaving only the perimeter tiles to cut and fit. With self-adhesive vinyl tiles the backing paper is partially removed and the tile is accurately positioned on one edge pressing it against its neighbour. Then the backing paper is completely removed and the tile is pressed down with a cloth pad working from this initial edge and ensuring that air is excluded.

With cork and ceramic tiles, first adhesive must be spread with a notched trowel to cover about 1 m² at a time. Cork tiles must be butted as closely as possible, while ceramic tiles are spaced to allow grouting later. Most ceramic floor tiles are self-spacing, but some must be spaced using plastic spacers as used for wall tiles.

To mark border tiles for cutting, place the tile to be cut exactly over the adjacent last complete tile. Take a spare full tile and place this against the skirting so it partially covers the tile to be cut. Run a pen or pencil along the edge of the marking tile to mark the cutting line. Plastic tiles are best cut with scissors, cork tiles with a sharp trimming knife, and ceramic tiles by scoring and snapping as ceramic wall tiles; see pages 56 and 57.

To fit tiles around awkward shapes in doorways, either use a shape tracer tool, make a cardboard pattern, or use an adaption of the technique used to mark the border tiles, as shown in the diagrams overleaf.

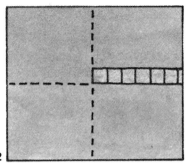

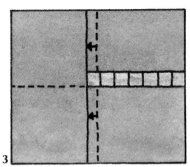

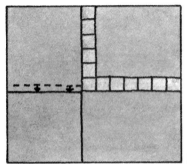

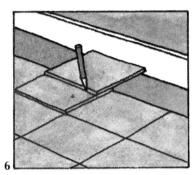

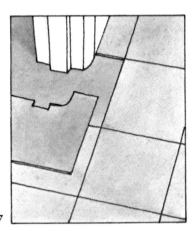

Tile floor coverings

1. Snap string lines across the floor to mark the centre point and give accurate guide lines for tile laying

2. Now lay a trial row of tiles, without adhesive, in row from the centre point

3. If the last tile will be less than half a tile wide move the string chalk line half a tile off centre and remark the line

4. Next check the tile layout in the other direction and if necessary move the guide line by half a tile width

5. If the tiles need separate adhesive, spread this with a serrated spreader to cover about 1 m². Work from the centre point of the room laying the tiles in the sequence shown here filling one segment at a time

6. To cut border tiles, place the tile to be cut exactly over the last full tile. Place another full tile against the skirting board to partially cover the tile to be cut. Run a pencil along the overlap to mark the cutting line. When the border tile is cut the tile will fit exactly into the space against the skirting

7. Cut a cardboard template to make it easy to fit tiles into awkward shapes such as around door architraves

8. Self-adhesive tiles will stick to a smooth surface, such as hardboard. In this case, remove the backing paper or plastic and smooth each tile down working from one edge which is butted up against the previously laid tile. Smooth each tile with a duster to exclude air bubbles

Ceiling repairs

Flaking surface

This is almost certainly due to an earlier application of distemper. Soak the ceiling with hot water and detergent and then scrape off the distemper. Wash the ceiling twice to remove all traces of the paint. When the surface is dry there should be no powder on your hand when you rub it across the surface. If there is still a powdery deposit, then paint the surface of the ceiling with a stabilising solution or a primer-sealer.

Hairline cracks

These are common and are usually nothing to worry about. Fill the largest cracks with a cellulose plaster filler, wherever possible raking along the cracks with the edge of a filling knife to give a good key for the filler. Make sure the filler is smoothed off to save rubbing-down later. Next, after ensuring the ceiling is clean and dry, cover the surface by lining it with plain or embossed lining paper (see overleaf), or paint it with a self-texturing compound. Alternatively, cover the ceiling with tiles or install a suspended ceiling (see page 72).

Deeper cracks

Tap the ceiling along the crack to ensure that the plaster around the damaged area is still firm. If it is not, chip it away until firm plaster is reached. Use the edge of the filling knife to form a V-shaped cavity above the crack and then press cellulose filler into the crack. If there are a lot of cracks to repair it will be cheaper to use a proprietary plaster, such as Sirapite. In this case the crack must be dampened with water before the filler is applied. A small hand-held garden trigger sprayer is ideal for applying the water.

Cracks that re-open need a reinforced repair using decorator's cotton scrim, which looks like a strip of open-mesh bandage. Repair the crack with filler and when this is dry use wallpaper paste to fix the scrim over the repair. Now either cover the entire ceiling with lining paper before redecorating, or cover just the repairs with lining paper. The paper should be about 300 mm wide and a section only about 150 mm wide down the centre is pasted. This is applied to the ceiling to cover the scrim and it is left to dry. The edges which are hanging down are then carefully torn off to leave a feathered edge which can be further disguised with fine surface filler before the ceiling is painted.

Cracks that re-open where the ceiling joins the wall are best covered by fixing plaster or expanded polystyrene cove here.

Repairing a hole in plasterboard ceiling. Use a padsaw to cut around damaged area

Cut back to the centre of joists above

Place plasterboard in hole and secure with plasterboard nails driven into the joists

Ceiling decoration

Papering

Erect two step-ladders and a scaffold board to enable you to reach the ceiling easily. Prepare the ceiling in the same way that walls are prepared for papering. Start papering close to the main window, hanging the strips parallel with the window wall. Use a chalked line to strike a straight line across the ceiling, allowing for about 10 mm to turn down on to the adjacent wall if the walls are to be papered. Paste each length and fold the paper concertina fashion, paste-side to paste-side. Use a part roll to support the folded paper, then unfold the first portion of paper and align it with the chalk line on the ceiling. Brush it on to the ceiling, working from the centre to the edges, then work along the ceiling unfolding the paper and brushing it on to the ceiling as you go.

Painting

Plan the job so you can complete the work in one session without breaks. Start in the corner nearest the window and work across the ceiling away from the light, painting in bands about 500 mm wide. Paint pads and rollers are the fastest tools for painting a ceiling using emulsion paint. Even the best rollers tend to splatter paint, a problem that is not found with paint pads or conventional brushes. If using a roller or paint pad it will be necessary to use a small brush to apply a narrow band of paint around the perimeter of the ceiling. After loading the roller evenly from a paint tray it is used in a random criss-cross fashion. A paint pad can be loaded straight from the tin and it is used gently, almost with a scrubbing action. If a brush is used, after spreading the paint it should be drawn lightly over the surface in one direction to obtain an even finish.

Texturing

Some texturing compounds are ready-mixed and self-texturing – they are applied by brush or roller and this automatically leaves a stippled surface. Other compounds of this type have to be mixed and are then applied by brush, after which they are given a texture as required using a sponge wrapped in polythene, a deeply textured roller, a smooth roller, a swirling comb, and so on.

Fixing ceiling cove

Adhesive is buttered onto the back of polystyrene cove

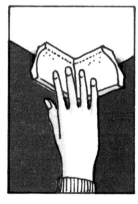

Pre-formed corner piece fixed in place

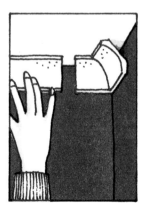

Lengths of cove are pushed firmly into place, butting-up at edges

Excess adhesive is used to fill gaps at cove edges

Tiling

The technique is the same for expanded polystyrene, fibreboard and cork tiles. The surface must be clean and dry and the correct adhesive must be used. Find the centre of the ceiling by stretching a string line from the centre points of opposite walls. Tiling should begin where the lines intersect, but a fixture such as a fluorescent light fitting may mean that the starting point has to be moved slightly. The starting point may also have to be moved half a tile's width to one side if only an ugly narrow strip of tiles will be left at the perimeter. Make sure that the adhesive is spread over the entire back of each tile before it is pressed into place. A square of hardboard will protect the surface of polystryene tiles when these are applied. Marking-out and cutting the perimeter tiles is as for floor tiles – see page 68.

Timber cladding

Tongued, grooved and V-jointed (T, G & V) timber matchboarding is ideal for cladding a bathroom ceiling if adequately protected from moisture with three coats of varnish. The matchboarding can be fitted directly to the ceiling plaster, or if the plaster is in very bad condition it can be removed and the match-boarding fixed directly to the joists. In either case the nails fixing the matchboarding must pass into the ceiling joists, so if the plaster is left in place, first probe it to locate the joists, then mark their positions on the surface of the ceiling using pencil lines. Fit the boards with 25 mm long zinc-plated panel pins which should be driven at an angle through the root of each tongue – see page 58. Work from one side of the room tapping the boards into place with an offcut of board to protect the tongues.

Tiling a ceiling

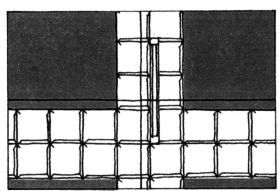

1. A ceiling to be tiled is marked out in the same way as a floor using chalked string lines. Tile from the central point, but make allowance for fixtures, like fluorescent lights

2. Coat the back of each tile with a suitable adhesive ensuring that the entire area is covered with the adhesive

3. Press the tile into place on the ceiling, making sure each tile is closely butted up to the neighbouring tiles. A square of hardboard will protect the surface of expanded polystyrene tiles

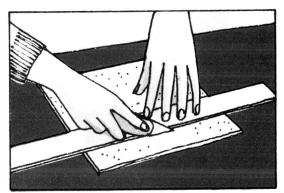

4. Around the perimeter of the ceiling, tiles must be trimmed to fit. In most cases the tiles will be soft enough to trim with a sharp knife

Suspended ceilings

Where a ceiling is in poor condition, or there are ugly pipes or beams in the surface of the ceiling, or the ceiling is just too high then it can be a good idea to build a suspended ceiling. Remember that the minimum recommended ceiling height is 2.3 m.

There are two basic types; a lightweight aluminium-framed suspended ceiling that can be fitted either with conventional fibreboard panels, or with translucent plastic panels which can be illuminated from above to give an overall spread of lighting; or a traditional type of suspended ceiling can be made using a timber framework which can be surfaced either with plasterboard sheets, which will make it indistinguishable from a conventional ceiling, or with timber cladding. Both methods allow the easy installation of a modern lighting system using downlighters or spotlights.

Kits are available for making a lightweight suspended ceiling. Aluminium angle sections are fixed around the perimeter of the room at the desired ceiling height and a grid of aluminium frames are fixed between these main sections with wires from the ceiling to give some support. The ceiling panels simply rest on the grid. These panels are available in a number of styles.

A timber suspended ceiling can be made by fixing 100 mm × 50 mm wall plates to walls on opposite sides of the room across the minimum span, and then further 100 mm × 50 mm joists at 450 mm centres can be notched into the wall plates to form a new ceiling. Plasterboard or tongued and grooved timber cladding is nailed directly to this framework.

Above: fixing aluminium sections for a lightweight illuminated ceiling around the perimeter of the room at the desired ceiling height. Normally the sections can be fixed with masonry nails driven home with a nail punch
Right: a grid is made up from various aluminium sections fixed between the perimeter supports. Across wide spans wires can be fixed from the ceiling to prevent the sections from sagging

Electrics   by Geoffrey Burdett

In the wrong hands, or incorrectly installed, electricity and a bathroom can be a fatal combination. However, if you follow the advice given here you will ensure that your wiring system complies with the latest wiring regulations and then you can be sure that your installation will be perfectly safe.

Remember to *switch off* at the mains supply before undertaking any electrical work, and then before touching any bare wires double-check with a mains-tester screwdriver that the wires are, in fact, dead. *Never take chances*. If you have any doubts on your competence at wiring, then call in a qualified electrician to carry out this stage of the work.

Lighting

Lighting fittings in bathrooms must not be pendants with flexible cords. They should be close-mounted non-pendant fittings, preferably totally enclosed. Where the light is an open-batten lampholder it must have a deep skirt, termed an HO (Home Office) skirt, so that the metal cap of the bulb cannot be touched until the bulb is parted from the lampholder contact pins.

Switches for the lights must be out of reach of anyone using the bath or shower. To eliminate any risk of electrocution, the lighting switch should be cord-operated, the insulated cord of which need not be out of reach of a person using the bath.

All other switches, except that of a BS3052 shaver supply unit, must be out of reach from the bath or shower.

Wiring for fluorescents

The circuit wiring for fluorescent lights is the conventional wiring as used for ordinary lights with tungsten-filament bulbs. Since, however, a fluorescent fitting has no live loop-in terminal or facilities for the circuit live feeds, it is better to wire the fluorescent light, but not necessarily the whole circuit, on the joint box method (see below and page 76). With this method the circuit-feed cable, comprising a twin and earth pvc-sheathed cable, is run to a joint box from either another joint box or from a loop-in ceiling rose.

The feed cable is run to a convenient position in the ceiling void or in the loft fairly near to the point of the live end of a linear fluorescent fitting or just above a circular fluorescent fitting.

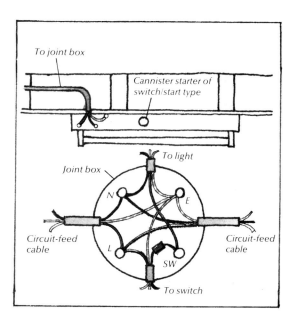

Fluorescent lighting – diagrams of connections at joint box where a light is wired on the joint box method. (Note: broken line indicates green/yellow earth sleeving.)

73

From the joint box a length of the same cable is passed through the ceiling and into the fitting. Another length of the cable is run from the joint box to the switch position, which must be a cord-operated ceiling switch. (Under no circumstances may an ordinary dimmer switch be used to control an ordinary fluorescent light.)

Fluorescent fittings have a terminal block containing live and neutral terminals and also earthing facilities.

There are two types of linear fluorescent fitting. One is the switch-start type, the other is non-switch-start, sold under trade names such as Quick-start and Instant start. These have no starter switch and earthing is essential to assist in starting. Also a switchless fluorescent fitting must have a special type of tube which has a metal strip running throughout its length, or it should have a special coating. The switch-start type can have either a switch-start type tube or a quick-start tube.

Circular and miniature fluorescent lights are all of the switch-start type and contain a starter canister.

Tungsten lights

There are no special problems associated with tungsten filament lights, these having either ordinary (GLS) electric light bulbs or special bulbs or tubes. Ceiling fittings are normally loop-in batten lampholders and some close ceiling fittings have loop-in facilities (right and page 76). Wall lights, when required, are best wired on the joint box method so that only one twin and earth sheathed cable is run down the wall to the light which in any event has no loop-in facilities.

Spotlights

Spotlights are not really suitable for the bathroom as they cannot readily be adjusted because they must be out of reach of a person using the bath or shower and they could be adversely affected by condensation. However,

they are worthy of mention as they could be wanted in a cloakroom.

A spotlight is an adjustable lighting fitting containing a reflector lamp or a PAR 38 lamp. A single fitting can be fixed to a wall or ceiling and mounted on a round metal box termed a BESA box fixed to the surface of the ceiling or sunk flush. Spotlights are supplied fitted with a short length of 3-core circular sheathed flexible cord, white or black, which is connected to the circuit conductors within the BESA box.

Two or more spotlights can be fixed to a lighting track. Wiring to the lights or track is conventional.

Downlighters

A downlighter is a form of spotlight directing light downwards. Basically a downlighter is a plastic cylinder which is produced in three main versions, flush, semi-recessed and surface. The flush type is preferred in the home and is designed for fitting into the ceiling void beneath the floorboards.

ISL (internally silvered reflector) lamps are usually fitted into a downlighter. Downlighters can be fixed in any position where a pool or

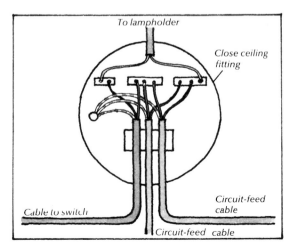

Tungsten lights – loop-in method

pools of light are required. In some versions the lampholder assembly is adjustable for directing the downward light in various angles including wallwashing where pools of light are thrown on to a wall. Circuit wiring is conventional, using the joint box method.

Installing a downlighter

First check that there is sufficient depth in the ceiling void. A typical downlighter has a depth of 170 mm and can be accommodated in most ceiling voids for these usually have a joist depth of 225 mm.

Pierce a hole in the ceiling to coincide with the centre of the downlighter. Raise the floorboard above to check whether the down-lighter will clear the joists. If necessary alter the position to clear the joists. Mark a circle of the required diameter in the ceiling. Cut the hole and fix the downlighter in accordance with the makers' instructions. Connect the circuit cable to the downlighter terminals and fit the ISL lamp.

Where a loft is above the bathroom ceiling, as in a bungalow, it will be necessary to protect the fitting by enclosing it in timber.

Alcove striplights

Striplights for fitting in alcoves and under cupboards may be either the tungsten-filament type or mini-fluorescent.

Tungsten-filament striplighting is cheaper to buy because unlike fluorescent lights no ballast gear and starter is needed. However, miniature fluorescent tubes are of very low wattage and much less costly to run than tungsten and the tubes last very much longer.

As striplights have no loop-in facilities the circuit wiring should be on the joint box method with one cable only going to each light. If a number of striplights are to be controlled from the one pullcord switch, wiring is simple, but if each is to be switched individually the wiring can be complicated.

Over-mirror striplight

An over-mirrror striplight (see diagram below) is designed for directing light on to the face when shaving (or for make-up). The striplight is a complete lighting fitting which in the bathroom must have the lamp completely enclosed and the lampholders shielded when changing a lamp.

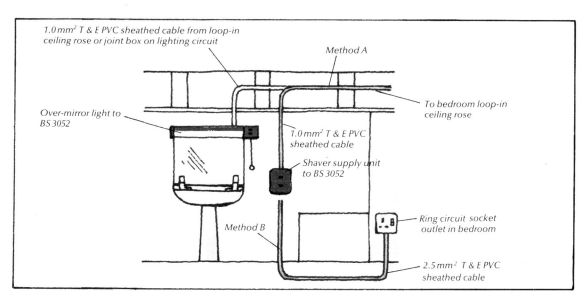

1.0 mm² T & E PVC sheathed cable from loop-in ceiling rose or joint box on lighting circuit

Method A

Over-mirror light to BS 3052

To bedroom loop-in ceiling rose

1.0 mm² T & E PVC sheathed cable

Shaver supply unit to BS 3052

Method B

Ring circuit socket outlet in bedroom

2.5 mm² T & E PVC sheathed cable

Over-mirror striplight and shaver socket. Note: over-mirror light and shaver socket in bathroom must be to BS 3052. A shaver supply unit must also be to BS 3052. This diagram shows alternative methods of wiring a shaver supply unit; A from lighting circuit and B as spur from ring circuit

A version having a shaver socket is also available which for installation in the bathroom must be made to BS 3052 and contain an isolating transformer to provide a non-earthed supply to the socket. The fitting should have a cord-operated switch for the light.

Moving a light

To move a fixed light from one position to another it is necessary first to take down the lighting fitting to get at the circuit wires. If there is more than one cable with two conductors (plus any earth conductors) this indicates that the light is wired on the loop-in method. Note which wires are connected to the flex terminals of the fitting and which are not as the latter are live feed wires. Tie jointed wires together so they do not separate.

Draw the cables back into the void and connect them to a joint box fixed between two joists, having first raised a floorboard if not in the loft. Pierce a hole in the ceiling at the new position of the light and if necessary raise a floorboard above it. From the joint box run a length of 1.0^2 twin and earth PVC-sheathed cable to the new position. Fix a piece of wood batten between the joists against the ceiling, having first drilled a hole in the batten for the cable.

Prepare the end of the cable and connect and fix the light. Connect the other end of the cable to the joint box, the red and black conductors to the terminals containing the wires labelled Flex. Restore the power.

Adding a light

When adding a light to be controlled by its own switch, locate the nearest loop-in ceiling rose from which the cable for the new light can be looped (page 74). From this light position run a length of $1.0 \, mm^2$ twin and earth PVC-sheathed cable either to a joint box or direct to the new light if this is to be a loop-in fitting.

If a joint box system is used, fix a 4-terminal box about midway between the new light and its switch. Fix the box to a timber batten between two joists. From the joint box run two lengths of the same cable, one length to the new light, the other to its switch. If a loop-in light, run a length of the same cable from the light to its switch. Connect the lighting fitting to the circuit cables and fix it to the ceiling.

If a wall light is being fitted, first fix a backing box flush into the wall to house a cable connector and the unsheathed ends of the wires. Then fix the cord-operated switch and connect the switch as shown below.

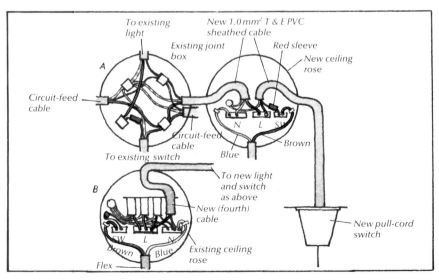

Adding a light and switch by looping out of (A) a joint box or (B) a loop-in ceiling rose

Other electrical fittings

Wiring for water heaters

A washbasin water heater, usually instantaneous, has a loading of 3 kW. Thermal storage water heaters also have a loading of 3 kW. These water heaters can be supplied from spurs connected to a ring circuit.

For a 3 kW water heater supplied from a spur, locate the nearest ring circuit socket for looping. From this socket run a length of 2.5 mm² twin and earth PVC-sheathed cable to a switched fused connection unit fixed on the wall near the water heater. Connect the water heater to the switched fused connection unit with 1.5 mm² 3-core flexible cord. The switched fused unit must be out of reach of a person using the bath or shower. Where this is impracticable it is necessary to fit a non-switched fused connection unit next to the socket outlet from which the spur is taken and from it run a length of 1.5 mm² twin and earth PVC-sheathed cable to a cord-operated double-pole switch with neon indicator above the washbasin water heater and from it run a length of the same cable down to the water heater.

Shaver socket

A shaver socket for installation in a bathroom must be that of a shaver supply unit made to British Standards (BS) 3052 and containing an isolating transformer and a current-limiting device.

The unit may be supplied from a ring circuit spur or from the lighting circuit without needing any intervening fuse (page 75). If from a lighting circuit run a length of 1.0 mm² twin and earth PVC-sheathed cable from the nearest loop-in ceiling rose. If a ring circuit spur, use 2.5 mm² twin and earth cable run from a ring circuit socket outside the bathroom.

As the shaver supply unit is made to the requirements of a stringent BS, it may be fixed anywhere in the bathroom, even within reach of a person using the bath.

Wiring an extractor fan

An extractor fan has a loading of about 40 watts and should be supplied from the lighting circuit. Run a length of 1.0 mm² twin and earth PVC-sheathed cable from the nearest loop-in ceiling rose to a clock connector fixed on the

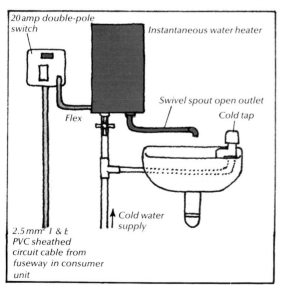

Circuit and control for an instantaneous water heater for a washbasin. The mains outlet should be a switched fused connection unit and the circuit cable should be a spur from a ring circuit

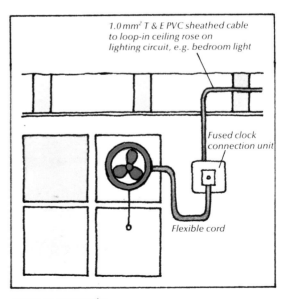

Wiring an extractor fan

wall in line with the fan. The fan is connected to the detachable fused section of the connector by 3-core sheathed flex. If the fan has no cord-operated switch, it is necessary to run the cable from the loop-in ceiling rose to a double-pole cord-operated ceiling switch fixed near the fan and connected to it by twin and earth PVC-sheathed cable.

Electric space heaters

Any electric heater installed in a bathroom must be fixed, i.e. requiring tools to move it. The heater may be fixed to the wall or floor.

Radiant heater

One of the most commonly used bathroom heaters is the radiant wall reflector heater. This type has one or more silicon glass enclosed spiral-wire elements protected by a metal guard and controlled by a pull-cord integral switch (see below). A heater with this type of element must in addition be controlled by an independent double-pole switch fixed within reach of the heater. The circuit for the heater can be a spur off a ring circuit, and needs a fuse to protect the heater.

The heater should be installed on the opposite wall to the bath, out of reach of a person using the bath. The mains outlet can be a switched fused connection unit with flex outlet so providing the necessary fuse and double-pole switch. The connection unit is fixed next to the heater and therefore out of reach of the bath and left switched on, except when attending to the heater to replace an element or when cleaning the reflector. The heater is fitted with 3-core flexible cord which is connected to the fused connection unit.

Oil-filled radiator

To heat a bathroom for long periods, even when it is not being used, a floor- or wall-mounted thermostatically controlled oil-filled radiator is a good choice. This may be supplied from a switched fused connection unit fixed near the radiator provided it is out of reach of a person using the bath. Otherwise fit a non-switched fused connection unit next to the ring circuit socket outside the bathroom from which the spur cable is run (see below). Fix a cord-operated double-pole switch on the bathroom ceiling, run a cable from the switch down the wall to a flex outlet unit fixed near the radiator and connect the flex of the radiator to the outlet unit.

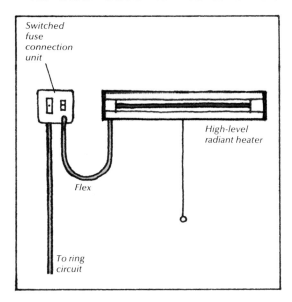

Radiant wall reflector space heater. Note: heater must be fixed to be out of reach from the bath and on the opposite wall to the bath

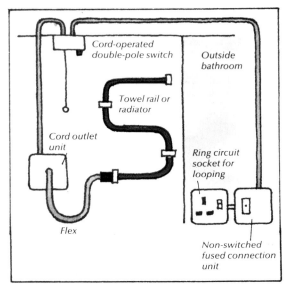

Wiring a heated towel rail or oil-filled radiator

Heated towel rail

The simplest towel rail is an S-shape plastic rod containing an embedded element and mounted at an angle of 90 degrees. This, like an oil-filled radiator, is connected either to a cord outlet unit or to a switched fused connection unit. The heater not only keeps towels dry and warm, but can provide sufficient heat to combat condensation.

Instantaneous shower

A shower unit has a 6 kW or a 7 kW element switched on by a pressure switch actuated by the pressure of the inflow of cold water when the inlet valve is turned on. Since the electric current is flowing only when the water is passing over the element, there is no heat loss through stored hot water.

A 30 amp circuit (see below) consisting of 6.0 mm^2 twin and earth PVC-sheathed cable is required for the shower unit. The circuit cable originates at a 30 amp circuit fuse or m.c.b. (miniature circuit breaker) in a consumer unit or in a switchfuse unit connected separately to the mains by the electricity board.

At the shower unit end a 30 amp double-pole isolating switch is required. This switch should be in close proximity to the shower unit, but as a wall-mounted switch must be out of reach of a person using the fixed bath or shower, it is better, and is now common practice, to fit a cord-operated ceiling switch. Such a switch has been designed for the purpose, has a current rating of 30/45 amps, contains a pilot lamp and is fixed to a 1-gang plastic box.

When installing the circuit, run the cable from the consumer unit or switchfuse unit up into the ceiling void or loft above the bathroom to the point above where the ceiling switch is to be fixed. From this position run another length of the same cable down the bathroom wall to the shower unit, allowing sufficient cable for connection within the unit.

Pierce a hole in the ceiling at the switch position. Fix a piece of wood batten between the joists above this hole as fixture for the switch, having drilled a hole in the batten coinciding with the hole in the ceiling.

Thread the cables through the hole. Knock out the section of thin plastic in the base of the box, thread in the cable, and fix the box to the timber using gauge No. 8 woodscrews. Prepare the ends of the cables and connect them to the switch. Fix the switch to its box using the screws supplied.

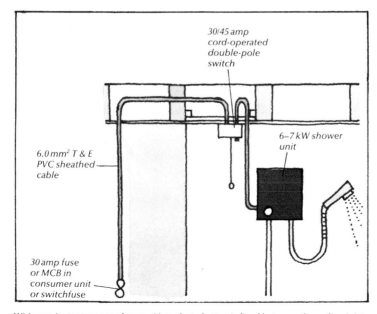

30/45 amp cord-operated double-pole switch

6–7 kW shower unit

6.0 mm^2 T & E PVC sheathed cable

30 amp fuse or MCB in consumer unit or switchfuse

Wiring an instantaneous shower. Note that a batten is fixed between the ceiling joists as a mounting for the switch box

Plumbing

Pipes: types and sizes

Supply pipes

These carry water to the fittings. In an old house they could be made of lead, but nowadays in almost all cases the supply pipes will be of copper. Because it is very difficult to make connections with lead pipe it is best to replace it with copper tube, if possible removing all the lead so that the plumbing system will be copper right from the mains stopcock. This is found where the service pipe enters the house, usually under the kitchen sink. This connection could need a lead-to-copper joint, which is the one connection that should be made by a plumber.

Copper tube is commonly found in three sizes: 15 mm, 22 mm and 28 mm. These tubes are equivalent to the old imperial sizes of ½ in, ¾ in, and 1 in. They are not exact conversions because the metric tube is measured according to the external diameter of the tube, while the imperial tube which was made pre-1971 was measured according to its internal diameter. In practice this means that old and new tubes vary slightly in diameter. Of course, if all new pipes and pipe fittings are used to connect the bathroom fittings there will be no problems, except at the joints where they connect up with the existing system. If compression pipe fittings are used, these will work with both old and new copper tube in the 15 mm and 28 mm sizes. Where a 22 mm compression fitting is to connect with a ¾ in pipe, an adaptor will be needed.

With capillary fittings, where a snug fit is critical for a good soldered joint, adaptors are needed in all sizes when connecting metric tubing to the older imperial tube. In a bathroom it is very likely that you will find ¾ in or 22 mm tubing because this is normally used for hot and cold water supply.

Plastic 15 mm, 22 mm and 28 mm tubing has now been approved for hot and cold supply pipes. The advantages are that plastic pipe is light and easy to handle, is easy to join using Acorn push-fit fittings or solvent cement (no blowtorches), and fittings are neat. The pipe has good thermal insulation, reducing heat loss and surface condensation. Transition fittings are available for connecting a plastic system to traditional threaded, soldered or compression fittings. At the time of writing, a plastic system is roughly comparable in price to a copper, but unlike copper pipe, plastic pipe, while being flexible, cannot be bent and bends must be formed using a combination of elbow and bend fittings.

Waste pipes

Copper and lead have been used for the waste pipes from bathroom fittings, but almost invariably new work is done using plastic waste pipes. Although these pipes are based on the old imperial 1¼ in and 1½ in inside diameters, each manufacturer's fittings tend to vary slightly in size and therefore you should choose one make and stick to it throughout. Most systems use push-fit joints with integral O-rings to make a seal. Alternatively, Multi-Joint fittings can be used which have compression-type rings enabling connections to be made to all types of plastic, and copper and lead waste pipes.

Drain pipes

The main soil stack, whether a two-pipe or a single-stack system, used to be a 4 in cast-iron pipe, while the underground part used to be glazed stoneware. Nowadays, the above-ground part is push-fit plastic while the underground part may be stoneware with plastic push-fit joints, push-fit plastic or occasionally pitch-fibre.

Know your plumbing system

Your plumbing system can be divided into three distinct parts: the cold water supply, the hot water supply, and the drainage system. If you have a hot water radiator central-heating system, this is a fourth plumbing system, but this should not be affected by bathroom improvements and is not covered here.

Study the diagrams overleaf and get to know how your system compares with the examples and this will enable you to plan how best to connect the new fittings and make it easy for you to shut off the water to the bathroom while the connections are made.

An easy way to tell which taps are mains-supplied and which are served from a storage cistern is to turn off the water at the mains stop cock. Mains-fed taps will be without water once the rising main has drained (after about one minute), while cistern-fed taps will run for a long period until the cistern is emptied.

The ideal system has a cold-water storage cistern in the loft, giving sufficient head of water for a shower and equal pressure in both hot and cold water supply pipes to make shower, bath and basin mixer taps easy to connect. Problems arise where the hot or cold taps are mains-fed and when the cold-water storage cistern is mounted in the airing cupboard, just above the hot water cylinder.

Installing the fittings becomes much easier if parts of the plumbing system can be isolated, so a first job could be to fit gate valves in the supply pipes so that individual pipes can be shut off without disruption to entire household water supply.

Drainage system

With modern tubes and pipe fittings it is easy to adapt and extend the water-supply pipes, but altering the drainage system is another matter. As previously mentioned, wherever possible try to group fittings around the existing soil stack so that they can be connected into it.

If it is a single-stack drainage system (see page 16) it is important to follow the design rules laid down for this type of drainage. All fittings should have 75 mm (3 in) deep-seal traps, all the waste pipes should be kept as short as possible with as shallow a fall as possible. Basin and bidet wastes can be in 1¼ in nominal inside diameter (32 mm nominal outside diameter) pipe, but bath and shower wastes should be in 1½ in nominal inside diameter (40 mm nominal outside diameter) pipe. Because of the risk of siphoning out, 1¼ in pipes should be no more than 1.68 mm (5½ ft) long. If the waste has to be longer than this, use 1½ in pipe. To reduce the number of connections that have to be made into a soil stack, remember that a basin waste, for example, can be run into a bath waste using a Tee fitting. If a waste connection has to be made into a plastic soil stack, a strap boss can be used. Remember that the local building control officer has to be consulted about changes to drainage systems and he will in any case probably specify how the changes should be made.

With ground-floor WCs there will probably be very little advantage in connecting the new pan to the soil stack. It will probably be just as easy to use a plastic underground system, and run a new drain into the nearest inspection chamber (see pages 15 and 16). With an old two-pipe system, bath, shower, basin and bidet wastes are very easy to take straight through an outside wall to discharge directly into a hopper head (see page 15).

Downstairs basins and shower trays can discharge into an external gulley, in which case the end of the waste pipe should be below the grating, but above the water level in the gulley. This arrangement is suitable whether the house has a single-stack or two-pipe drainage system. See illustration overleaf for water supply systems, and the illustrations on pages 15 and 16 for drainage systems.

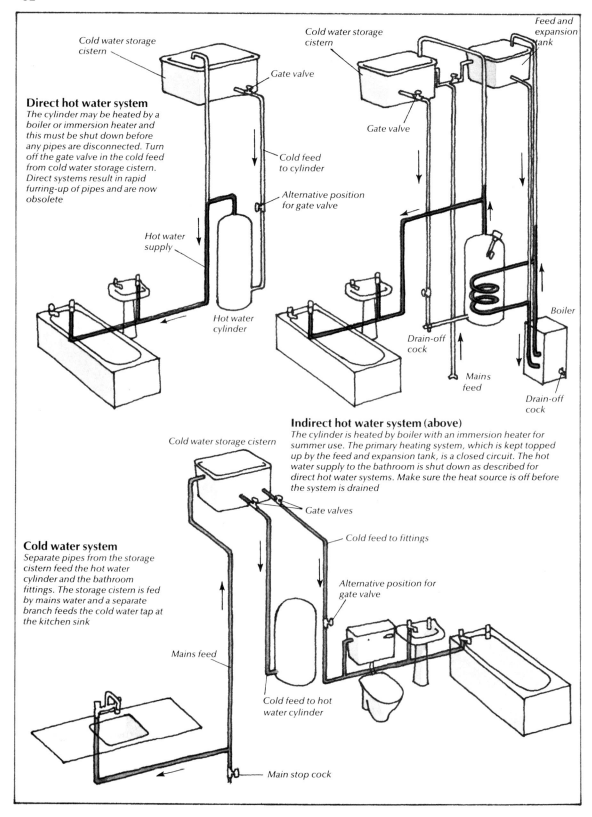

Direct hot water system
The cylinder may be heated by a boiler or immersion heater and this must be shut down before any pipes are disconnected. Turn off the gate valve in the cold feed from cold water storage cistern. Direct systems result in rapid furring-up of pipes and are now obsolete

Cold water storage cistern

Gate valve

Cold feed to cylinder

Alternative position for gate valve

Hot water supply

Hot water cylinder

Cold water storage cistern

Feed and expansion tank

Gate valve

Drain-off cock

Mains feed

Boiler

Drain-off cock

Indirect hot water system (above)
The cylinder is heated by boiler with an immersion heater for summer use. The primary heating system, which is kept topped up by the feed and expansion tank, is a closed circuit. The hot water supply to the bathroom is shut down as described for direct hot water systems. Make sure the heat source is off before the system is drained

Cold water storage cistern

Gate valves

Cold feed to fittings

Alternative position for gate valve

Cold water system
Separate pipes from the storage cistern feed the hot water cylinder and the bathroom fittings. The storage cistern is fed by mains water and a separate branch feeds the cold water tap at the kitchen sink

Mains feed

Cold feed to hot water cylinder

Main stop cock

Making joints

Copper tube

There are three types of fittings for joining copper tube. These are compression, soldered, and the push-fit type (see page 85).

Compression fittings. These brass fittings allow a mechanical joint to be made simply by using two spanners. Although this type does not look particularly neat, it is very easy to use and can be easily dismantled, which can be useful if it is likely a bathroom fitting may have to be moved in the future.

To make a joint with this type of fitting, just cut the end of the tube square using a fine hacksaw or a wheeled pipe cutter. The latter cuts pipe quickly and accurately and is not expensive – well worth buying if a bathroom is being improved and there are a fair number of pipes to be cut. It leaves the outside edge of the pipe smooth, but the inside edge of the pipe is turned in and this must be smoothed with a small file or the reamer which is often part of the pipe cutter.

If the pipe is cut by hacksaw, the outside edge of the pipe must be rounded-off with a file.

Slip the cap and olive (the compression ring) on to the pipe and after smearing some jointing compound like Boss White into the body of the fitting, push the pipe fully into the fitting as far as it will go. Push the olive and cap nut up to the fitting and then tighten the nut hand-tight. Repeat for the other side. Finally, using one spanner to hold the body of the fitting and the other on the cap nut, give each cap nut 1¼ turns. You cannot overtighten the cap nuts, but 1¼ turns beyond hand-tight will give a watertight joint, especially if jointing compound is used in the fitting. The latter is not essential but it does no harm.

Soldered fittings (also called capillary fittings). There are two types of fittings here – the solder-ring type and the end-feed type. Both look very neat, but they can only be removed by heating the pipe. The solder-ring type, which contains solder and merely needs to be heated, costs about half the price of the equivalent compression fitting. The end-feed type, which needs solder to be added when the joint is heated, is even cheaper at less than a quarter of the price of the compression fitting. Both types require heating with a blowtorch, so be very careful when working near combustible materials, particularly plastic bathroom fittings. In fact, use compression fittings in these situations.

These fittings are easy to use as long as the end of the pipe and inside of the fitting are scrupulously cleaned. The best way to clean the pipe is with a strip of emery cloth. Finally polish the pipe and inside of the fitting with fine steel wool until it shines and then put a smear of paste-flux on both surfaces.

Push the pipe into the fitting until it reaches the stop, then heat the fitting. A heat-resistant cloth can be placed behind the fitting to protect the background from the blowtorch flame. With a solder-ring fitting, continue to heat until a bright ring of solder appears all round the pipe. Take the heat away long before solder starts to drip out which indicates the joint has been overheated. With end-feed fittings, heat until the flux starts to melt then hold some solder wire at the point the tube enters the fitting and allow the solder to melt and be taken into the fitting. You will soon be able to judge when enough solder has been taken in, but as a guide a 15 mm fitting will need about a 15 mm length of solder and a 22 mm fitting will need about 22 mm of solder. When the joints have cooled, rub off flux with a rag and polish the pipe with wire wool.

Push-fit fittings. These are new, and not widely used at present. These plastic fittings (called Acorn fittings) will join copper tube in 15 mm and 22 mm sizes and can also be used with some types of plastic tube in similar sizes. The tube is cut square and the end is smoothed as for compression fittings, but in this case all that is necessary is to apply silicone lubricant to the tube and push it into the fitting as far as the stop. The pipe can be rotated after fixing, but it cannot be removed without dismantling the fitting. Price is a bit less than a standard brass compression fitting.

Plastic tube

Push fit. Cut the end of the pipe square and use a knife to remove burrs from inside the pipe.

Chamfer the end of the pipe to an angle of about 15 degrees using a file. Lubricate the end of the pipe with a little washing-up liquid and then push it into the fitting past the sealing ring and up to the stop. Mark the pipe at the mouth of fitting and then withdraw it about 9 mm which will allow for expansion. Some fittings like the Multi-Joint have a cap nut which tightens a rubber seal around the pipe like a compression fitting. In this case tighten the nut only hand-tight – do not use a spanner.

Solvent weld. Prepare the pipe as above. Clean the pipe and inside of the fitting with solvent cleaner. Immediately apply a liberal coat of solvent weld cement to the pipe and a sparing coat to the inside of the fitting. Push the pipe into the socket with a slight twisting motion. Make adjustments immediately. Wait an hour before using the pipework; four hours if a hot water system. If a joint leaks it has to be cut out and replaced with two connectors and a short length of pipe.

Bending tube

Plastic tube and drain pipes cannot be bent, but 90-degree and 135-degree bends are available which allows turns to be built-up.

Copper tube can be bent, although elbow fittings are best used for tight bends. The easiest method is to use a pipe-bending machine, which can be hired. This will make particularly easy work of bending 22 mm pipe which takes quite an effort to bend by hand. For both 15 mm and 22 mm pipe, bending springs are available. These are lightly greased and then slipped inside the tube. If an adequate length of tube is left, the pipe can then be bent around the knee. This should be done carefully to avoid forming kinks. To assist spring withdrawal, open the bend slightly and with a large nail through the ring in the spring, turn it clockwise while pulling firmly. After the spring has been withdrawn, the tube can be cut off close to the bend if this is where the bend is wanted.

An easier, though less attractive, solution to the problem of bending pipe is to use hand-bendable corrugated plumbing connectors. These tubes are available in 15 mm and 22 mm sizes and they will take compression or capillary fittings. The corrugations prevent the tube from collapsing when it is bent, and a bending spring is unnecessary.

Fitting taps

Taps, and other screwed fittings, such as ball valves, are still sold in imperial dimensions. That is ½ in for basin and bidet taps and mixers, and ¾ in for bath taps and mixers. However, when changing old taps for new ones, do check the tail length (the threaded portion). Formerly taps had 2½ in tails but now the British Standard is 50 mm (or almost 2 in). This can mean that, when taps are being changed, there will be a gap of about 12.5 mm between the tail and the tap connector. To bridge this gap Conex No. 74 adaptors in ½ in and ¾ in sizes are readily available.

Most taps will fit round or square holes in bathroom fittings, but check that the correct washers are used before fitting. Some types are anti-rotational. Make sure the taps are fitted symmetrically and that they both discharge into the fitting without splashing on to the ledge, or shelf.

It is a good idea to apply little non-setting mastic (such as Plumbers' Mait) to the underside

Working with pipes
1. Compression fittings. Step one: cut pipe square.
2. Step two: round-off outside of pipe and remove burrs with a file.
3. Step three: tube can be inserted into fitting without removing cap nut or olive, but usually it is better to slip these over the pipe with a smear of jointing compound over the end.
4. Step four: push the pipe fully into the fitting then tighten the cap nut (hand-tight, plus 1¼ turns).
5. Cross-section of compression fitting. As cap nut is tightened, the olive is compressed to form a watertight joint.
6. Soldered fittings. Step one: after cutting pipe square, clean end with emery cloth and polish with wire wool.
7. Step two: apply paste flux to end of pipe.
8. Step three: smear paste flux inside fitting then push pipe fully home. With solder ring type, as shown here, heat fitting until a bright ring of solder appears all round joint.
9. With end-feed type, step three is as above, but when flux starts to melt in heat apply solder wire at the point where the pipe enters the fitting.
10. Solder-ring capillary fitting (top) and end-feed capillary or soldered fitting (below). The latter type is the cheapest and neatest fitting for copper tube.
11. The Acorn plastic push-fit fitting for joining copper and plastic tube. To make a joint the tube is simply pushed into the fitting.
12. Bending tube: use either a pipe-bending spring (top left) which is pushed inside the pipe before bending, or use a hand bendable corrugated plumbing connector shown here with a tap connector end

85

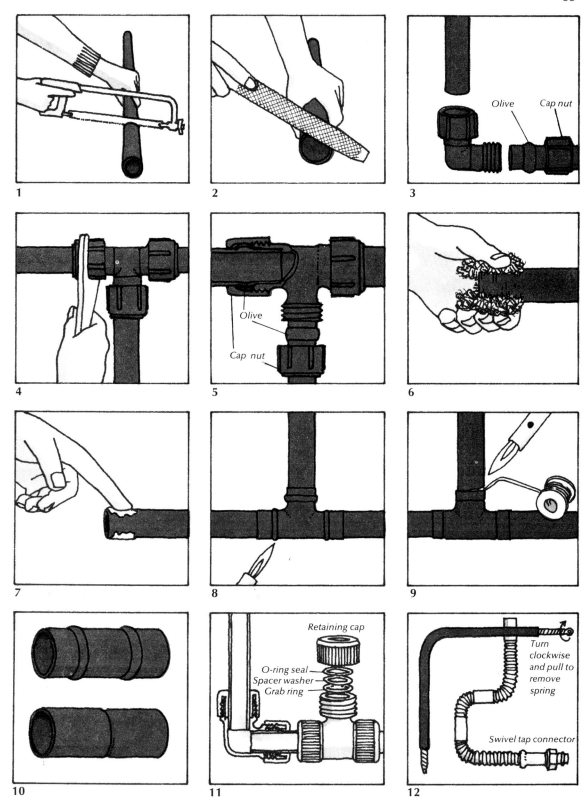

of each tap before installing it to prevent water from running into the fixing hole. The use of putty here is not recommended.

Be sure to fit the 'H' tap to the hot supply pipe and the 'C' to the cold. If there is a choice, as there is in a new installation, fit the 'H' tap to the left-hand side although there is no hard and fast rule here. If installed incorrectly, changing over the handles or, in cases where they are removable, simply the indices, will put things right.

Most mixers will replace a pair of individual taps, but check the distance between the tails of the mixer with the spacing of the holes on the fitting before buying. In most cases the hot and cold water supplies must be under equal pressure, which means that they should be fed from a storage tank.

To ensure a watertight joint, wrap the lower part of the threaded tap tail with three turns of PTFE tape before screwing the nut of the tap connector in place. Make sure this connector has a fibre washer on it that will seal against the end of the tap tail.

Fitting a WC

Removal of an old WC pan has been dealt with earlier – see page 52. The installation of a new WC pan has been made very easy by means of flexible WC pan connectors of which there are many types to suit the angle of the soil-pipe collar; the most comprehensive selection is the Multi-Kwik range. In an upstairs WC an offset pan connector will probably be required, while for a downstairs WC where the soil pipe is probably set in the floor, a bent connector will be used. In either case, lubricate the outlet on the pan with a little washing-up liquid on to the fins of the connector, remove the rags or newspapers which are temporarily blocking the soil pipe, and then lift the pan and connector assembly into place, pressing the fins on the connector into the soil pipe. With cast-iron soil pipes the connectors are designed to fit into the collars of pipes, but with stoneware pipes, where it is common for the collar to break off in

any case, the connector is designed to fit neatly into the pipe, replacing the collar.

When the pan is correctly positioned, fix it to the floor with brass screws. On a solid floor, the floor must be drilled with a long masonry bit so that plastic wallplugs can be inserted for the fixing screws. If you do not have a long-enough drill bit to drill through the fixing holes with the pan in place, the drill positions must first be marked and then the pan must be moved to allow the holes to be drilled.

Before screwing down the pan, check that it is level with a spirit level across the rim. If necessary pack under the pan with strips of lead, aluminium or hardboard. Fit plastic or rubber grommets under the screw heads and avoid overtightening the fixing screws, as this could crack the pan.

Low-level cistern with flush pipe

Fit the siphon assembly in the cistern with the rubber washers fitted as shown in diagram 1A opposite. The operating-lever assembly is fitted next (diagram 1D). When it comes to the ball-valve and overflow, a choice has to be made as to whether to have the conventional side supply and overflow, or bottom supply and overflow. If the cistern is a direct replacement

Fitting WCs
1. Fitting a low-level cistern with flush pipe. A – detail of siphon assembly connection. B – overflow connection. C – ball valve connection. D – operating lever assembly. E – flush pipe with rubber inlet connector inset.
2. By means of plastic pan connectors a standard horizontal outlet pan can be connected to most soil pipe positions. A – bent 'S' trap connector for ground floor pan. B – offset 'P' trap connector for upper floor pan. C – turned 'P' trap connector can be used on right or left hand. D – plan view of turned 'P' trap.
3. Fitting a close-coupled WC unit. A – detail of bottom inlet equilibrium ballvalve. B – lever assembly. C – detail of bottom inlet ballvalve connection. D – detail showing how cistern is attached to the back of the pan. E – detail of bottom outlet overflow connection.
4. Double-trap siphonic units. Basic assembly is as for a close-coupled WC with wing nuts and bolts to hold the cistern assembly firmly on the back of the pan. However, it is important to ensure that the lower end of the air tube in the siphon assembly enters the hole in the pan to seal off the aperture.
5. Wall-hung concealed cistern WC. The pan is mounted on sturdy support brackets fixed behind the partition wall. The cistern is also fixed behind the partition wall and is connected to the pan by means of a conventional flush pipe.
6. Back-to-wall concealed cistern WC. In this case the pan is fixed to the floor in front of an aperture which is cut in the partition wall. The cistern may be close-coupled (below) or connected to the pan by a flush pipe (type of pan shown at top)

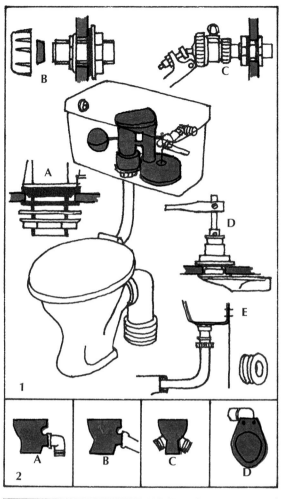

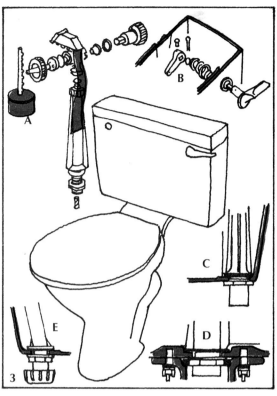

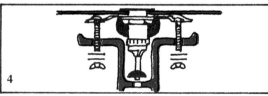

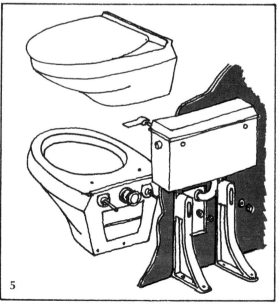

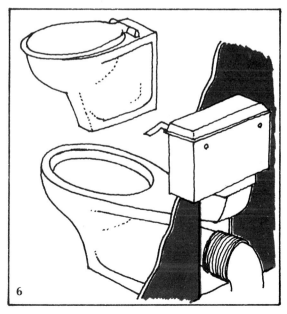

for an old cistern, it will be easiest to use the previous arrangement, but on a new installation it will look neatest to have bottom supply and overflow. In this case the water supply and overflow connections are made at the bottom of the cistern and the ball-valve and overflow units are on stems which take them above the water level in the cistern. As all the fittings will be in plastic, no jointing compound is needed and it is just a matter of getting the washers in the order shown on page 87. Most modern ball-valves are the quiet diaphragm/equilibrium types shown in the diagram on page 87. They are set to operate at normal water pressures of between 15 and 150 lb/in², but if the water pressure is very low the restrictor in the tail of the ball-valve should be removed.

The height to fit the cistern on the wall will be in the manufacturer's instructions. If this is not specified, use the flush pipe supplied as a guide. The base of the cistern is supported on metal hangers and one of these is fixed to the wall, then the cistern is placed in position, levelled and centralised, and the position of the other hanger marked together with the position of wall fixing holes through the cistern. Screw the cistern to the wall with brass screws.

Push a plastic or rubber inlet connector on to the flush pipe and after lubricating the connector with washing-up liquid push the assembly into the WC inlet (page 87), then connect the other end of the flush pipe to the outlet of the siphon in the cistern using the plastic cone in the capnut provided to make a watertight connection. Again, no jointing compound is necessary.

Use a 15 mm × ½ in straight or elbow copper to iron swivel tap connector to connect the water supply pipe to the tail on the ball valve. The swivel connector must be fitted with a fibre washer and the tail of the valve should be wrapped with three turns of PTFE tape to give a watertight joint.

Connect the overflow unit using a 22 mm push-fit plastic system making connections with suitable elbows and bends so that the pipe discharges through an outside wall. At the cistern a plastic capnut and cone makes a watertight joint. No jointing tape or mastic is required.

Close-coupled cistern

In this case the cistern rests on the back of the WC pan and is held in place by means of two fixing bolts attached to a coupling plate which is fixed to the underside of the cistern. A typical installation is illustrated on the previous page. A watertight seal is achieved by a thick rubber sealing washer which fits over the siphon assembly after the backnut has been tightened. Until the cistern is positioned against a wall there is a tendency for the entire unit to tip backwards, so be careful!

If a close-coupled WC is being connected to an existing soil pipe set in the floor, the position of the pipe will fix the distance that the back of the cistern comes from the wall. It may well be necessary to box-in behind the cistern with chipboard to ensure it is well supported.

Syphonic WC units

In this case fixing of the cistern is virtually the same as for an ordinary close-coupled cistern except that a special air-tube fitment fits on to the siphon tail. When the cistern is lowered on to the WC pan, care must be taken to ensure that the air tube enters the hole provided in the pan to seal off the aperture (diagram 4, page 87).

Concealed-cistern WC units

In this case the WC pan has to be fitted against a sturdy false wall faced with plywood or chipboard. Back-to-wall WCs are simply close-coupled units positioned against the false wall. Wall-hung units are bolted to strong support brackets bolted down against the back of the false wall and the pan is connected to the cistern by means of a flush pipe.

Fitting a washbasin

Most washbasins are the pedestal type. Fit the waste outlet and ½ in taps or mixers before lifting the basin on to the pedestal. Bed the waste outlet on plumbers' mastic and press it well down into the outlet hole so that the slot aligns with the built-in overflow. Put three turns of PTFE tape around the threaded part of the outlet, position the rubber washer on the waste followed by the metal connecting plate and then tighten up with the backnut. Taps are fitted as bath taps (see overleaf) and then the basin is lifted on to the pedestal to which it is secured with metal clamps. If the basin has screw holes, these should be used to fix the basin to the wall. Some basins are supplied with wall support brackets which attach to bolts fixed into holes in the underside of the pedestal flange using rubber cavity fixings (see diagram below). Metal brackets, which attach to the bolts using wing nuts, are screwed to the wall with 2½ in gauge 14 screws and wallplugs. For a neat appearance fit a 1¼ in bottle trap to the waste outlet, and 15 mm copper to ½ in iron elbow swivel tap

connectors so that the water supply pipes can be taken up behind the pedestal and across to the taps without being visible from the front.

If a pop-up waste is being fitted, usually the waste outlet is loosely assembled in the basin and then the pop-up waste body is tightened to the tail of the waste outlet. The operating arm of the waste is then turned to line up with the operating rod which goes through the back of the basin and then the backnut is tightened.

The advantage of wall-hung washbasins is that they can be fitted at any height, although 840 mm to the rim is normal. With the basin held at the desired height, mark the position of the fixing holes of the wall bracket on the wall, then remove the basin and bracket and drill the fixing holes. Fix the bracket securely and then fit the basin as described above.

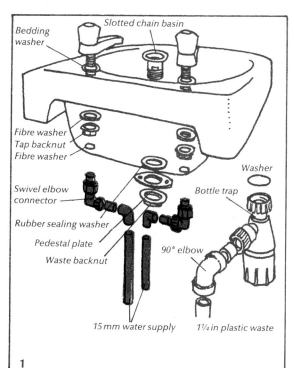

1. Plumbing connections to a typical washbasin with pillar taps.
2. Pedestal basin with three-hole mixer and pop-up waste.
3. Cross-section showing a typical method of fitting a basin with a chain waste to a pedestal. Note the bead of silicone sealant to prevent water from running between the outside of the basin and the pedestal.
4. Steadying brackets prevent basin from being pulled away from a wall.
5. In use, the fitting has a rubber sleeve which expands when tightened and holds the bracket in a hole moulded in the underside of the basin.
6. A pedestal basin fitted with the wall supports in place

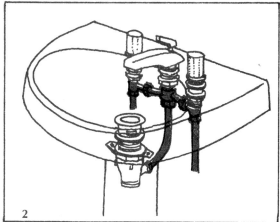

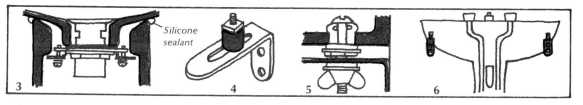

Fitting a bath

Removal of an old bath has been dealt with earlier – see page 52. Prepare the new bath for installation by assembling the feet. With a cast-iron bath this involves only clipping the feet into the lugs moulded into the base of the bath. Steel baths usually have cradle feet that attach to the base of the bath with bolts. When attaching these, be careful not to overtighten the bolts as this could distort the bath and chip the enamel.

Acrylic baths are normally moulded to a metal frame which supports the rim and they have a chipboard panel moulded to the base. The legs, which have adjustable feet, are screwed to the under-rim frame and to the base panel. On the larger baths there is often a smaller leg which screws in the middle of the base panel to support this area. Once the main legs are correctly positioned in the under-rim frame, they are screwed to the base panel, and care is needed here to ensure that pilot holes do not puncture the bath. Next the legs are fixed to the rim frame using self-tapping screws. A smear of petroleum jelly on these will make it easier to insert them.

Before lifting the bath into place, fit the waste outlet, overflow and taps. Put some plumbers' mastic under the rim of the waste outlet and wrap the thread of the outlet just below the slot with three turns of PTFE tape. Push the outlet into the position and attach the overflow collar, plastic washer and back nut according to the instruction sheet – the actual positioning of the components varies with the make of fitting. Long-nose pliers can be pushed into the waste outlet to stop it turning when the backnut is tightened. The overflow pipe has a sealing washer which is fitted before the overflow pipe is pushed from behind into the overflow outlet, allowing another sealing washer to be fitted and the overflow cover which has the chain attached to be screwed on. You can improvise a spanner for this job by pushing long-nose pliers into the slots in the overflow, allowing it to be turned easily.

Individual taps or bath mixers can be fitted next, seating them on the pliable gasket supplied and holding them in place with the backnuts. If a bath/shower mixer is fitted, remember that the cold supply must be taken from the same storage cistern as the hot supply and there must be an adequate head – see the section on fitting showers, page 93.

When taps are being fitted to steel baths, top hat washers must be placed over the tap tails before the back nuts are tightened. Without the top hat washers the taps will not fully tighten. As it is unlikely that the supply pipes will exactly match with the positions of the tap tails of the new bath, it is a good idea at this stage to fit short lengths of 22 mm tube to the tap tails using swivel tap connectors, or attach 22 mm hand-bendable connectors to the tails. Both methods will bring the connections away from the cramped under-rim area, making it easier to connect up the water supply pipes.

All types of baths are best rested on strong timber boards which can be screwed to the floor. On a timber floor these spread the load; on a solid floor they reduce the number of fixings that have to be made into the concrete floor. Lift the bath into place and adjust the feet so that the bath rim is perfectly level all round and check that the height of the rim will suit the bath panel. Check to see if a 75 mm deep 1½ in bath waste trap can be fitted to the waste outlet. This will involve cutting away the floor under the outlet, but a deep trap is efficient and it is essential if the waste is to be connected to a single-stack soil pipe. With a solid floor, as long as the bath is discharging into a gulley, a shallow-seal bath trap will be satisfactory. Also work out how the water supply pipes will be run so that pipes can be cut and bent before the bath is finally fitted. With acrylic and steel baths, mark on the floor the positions of the fixing holes in the feet. Acrylic baths usually have wall brackets and the positions of these should be marked on the wall.

Remove the bath to allow the necessary drilling and pipe installation to be carried out, then move it back into place again, check it for level, and finally screw the feet and wall brackets into place. Plastic baths may still flex if someone sits on the rim, but this can be prevented by screwing vertical timber battens to the wall at each end of the bath.

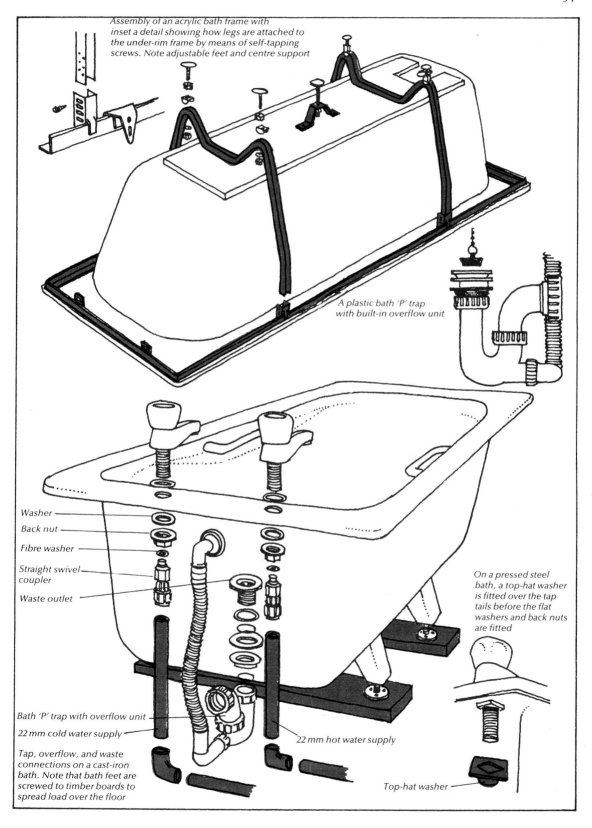

Assembly of an acrylic bath frame with inset a detail showing how legs are attached to the under-rim frame by means of self-tapping screws. Note adjustable feet and centre support

A plastic bath 'P' trap with built-in overflow unit

Washer

Back nut

Fibre washer

Straight swivel coupler

Waste outlet

On a pressed steel bath, a top-hat washer is fitted over the tap tails before the flat washers and back nuts are fitted

Bath 'P' trap with overflow unit

22 mm cold water supply

22 mm hot water supply

Tap, overflow, and waste connections on a cast-iron bath. Note that bath feet are screwed to timber boards to spread load over the floor

Top-hat washer

Fitting a shower

Without doubt the most efficient type of shower is the mixer type which uses cold water from the cistern in the loft mixed with hot water from the hot water cylinder. A separate shower mixer (ideally) or a bath/shower mixer can be supplied in this way and in the vast majority of houses the layout of the plumbing system will allow a shower mixer to be fitted. Diagrams 1 and 2 opposite show a typical system which is quite suitable for a shower. The hot and cold water supplies are both fed from the same storage cistern and the 'head', which is the vertical distance between the base of the cistern and the spray head of the shower, is a minimum of 1 m. If the head is less than this, standard 15 mm supply pipes will not give a sufficient flow of water for a satisfactory shower. Most mixers work best with a 1.5 m to 1.8 m head, although there are some (such as the Mira 915) that will work with a head as little as 600 mm. Note that the shower mixer has its own direct cold and hot water supplies. This ensures that the water supply to the shower does not fluctuate when other fittings are used. When it is impossible to arrange to have separate supply pipes in this way, a thermostatic mixer should be installed. In some old houses, the cold water storage cistern feeds the hot water cylinder, while the cold water supply is taken from the mains. This is unsuitable for a shower mixer (it is not good practice in any case), and new supply pipes should be taken from the cold water cistern to feed the mixer and the bathroom cold taps.

In an old or flat-roofed house or maisonette where there is insufficient head, the solution is to raise the cistern (diagram 3, opposite) or fit a pump (diagram 4).

Where the hot water comes from a storage unit having its own built-in cold water cistern and the cold taps are supplied direct from the rising main, there are two solutions illustrated in diagrams 5 and 6 opposite.

Another fairly common situation is when the hot water supply comes direct from the mains via a gas multi-point water heater and there is no stored supply. In some cases it may be possible to connect a shower mixer valve into the system as long as a water-pressure governor is installed in the cold main supply to reduce the hot and cold water supply pressures, but first check with the manufacturer of the shower valve or the water heater that the heater is suitable for this type of installation. If it is not, you can always fit an instantaneous electric shower unit.

The requirements for plumbing in an electric shower are illustrated in diagram 5 opposite. Only a 15 mm branch from the cold water rising main is required. The main requirement is make a safe electrical connection – see page 79.

The installation of a shower mixer or electric shower will be the same whether the shower is to be an over-bath type or have its own shower tray. Bath installation has been covered on page 90, and fitting a shower tray is also straight-forward and very similar. Fire-clay trays can be rested directly on the floor, in which case the waste pipe can be run between the floor joists to a suitable outlet. Alternatively, the tray can be raised in a sturdy framework of joists and a removable panel can be fitted at the side of the plinth to allow easy access to the waste outlet for maintenance from time to time.

Acrylic shower trays are supplied like baths on a supporting framework and in the same way the frame must be screwed to the wall and the feet to the floor. In all cases make sure that the rim of the shower tray is level all round.

Shower arrangements
1. Typical system using a bath/shower mixer.
2. System for separate shower mixer.
3. System with insufficient head (top) showing how cistern can be re-sited in loft and pipes extended to give the minimum 1 m head (bottom).
4. Where it is impossible to raise the cold water storage cistern, a shower booster pump can be fitted between the shower mixer valve and the shower rose.
5. Primatic-type hot water cylinder showing how to connect an instantaneous electric shower off the mains supply. See page 79 for electrical connections.
6. Alternative method of connecting a shower when a Primatic-type hot water cylinder is fitted. In this case a new small cold water storage cistern is fitted, together with a shower booster pump.
7. Shower mixer connected to a gas multi-point water heater.
8. Typical shower-tray installation. A new plasterboard stud wall conceals plumbing to shower mixer or electric shower (inset). The shower tray is raised above floor level on joists and an access panel allows maintenance to the 1½ in shallow seal trap and waste pipe which discharges into a convenient hopper head. Use a deep seal trap if waste discharges into a single stack soil pipe

93

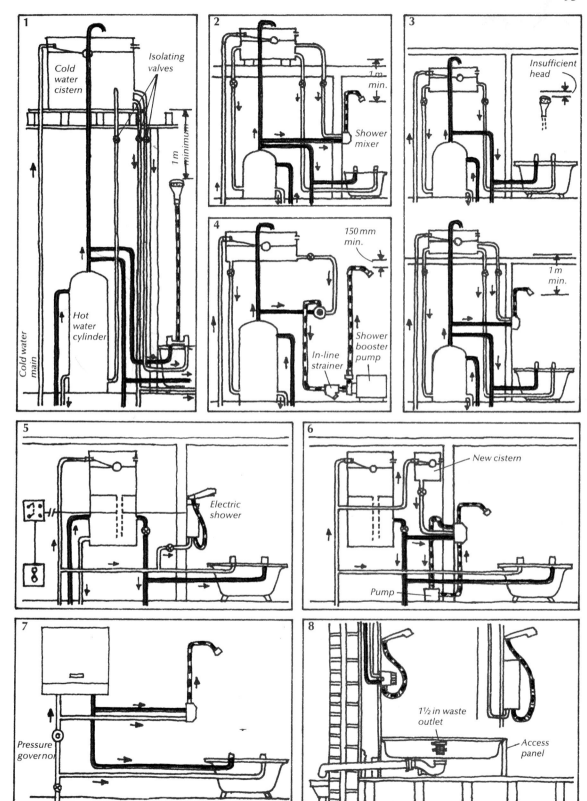

Installing a bidet

With an over-rim supply, plumbing is as easy as connecting a washbasin. The water supply can be taken via Tee connectors from the nearest hot and cold water supply pipes, probably those supplying the bath and basin.

The difficult type to connect is a rim-supply bidet with ascending spray. Once the bowl starts to fill with water the spray goes below water level and there is a risk that dirty water can be siphoned back into the household water supply. This type of bidet must be supplied from a storage cistern, *never* from the mains. Separate hot and cold 15 mm supply pipes must be run directly from the cold water cistern and from the hot cylinder without Tee-branches going to other fixtures. The minimum head of water required is 2750 mm (9 ft). This assumes the

bidet is more or less under the cistern; if a long run of pipework is unavoidable this head may have to be increased.

With both types the waste can be taken into the nearest waste pipe by means of a swept Tee-connector, or it can go direct to a hopper head or the soil stack. Like a washbasin, a bidet can have a plug waste, or pop-up waste. An intermediate type of bidet, less commonly seen, has a rim supply but no ascending spray and can be connected in the same way as an over-rim supply bidet.

1. Left: rim supply bidet with ascending spray. Right: over-rim supply bidet connected in the same way as a washbasin.
2. A rim supply bidet requires independent hot and cold feeds.
3. Connection of an over-rim supply monoblock bidet mixer with a pop-up waste fitting. These mixers usually have 12 mm plain copper tube inlets and 12 mm–15 mm reducing compression connectors are available for making the connections to the water supply. Shown at the bottom are the alternative waste traps that can be fitted to a bidet

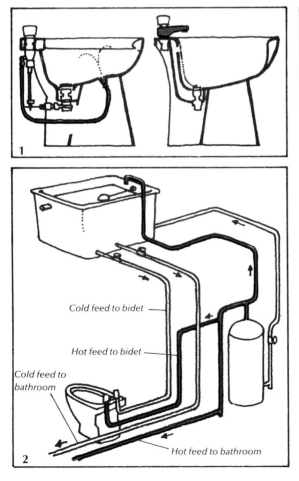

Cold feed to bidet
Hot feed to bidet
Cold feed to bathroom
Hot feed to bathroom

2

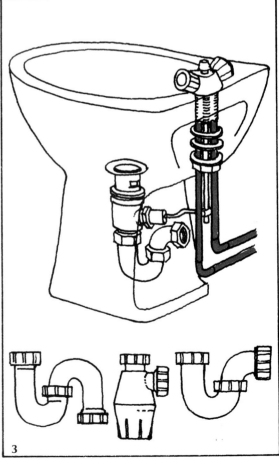

3

Bath panels

Moulded plastic panels are usually easy to fit. They simply push into plastic clips under the bath rim and attach by means of double-sided sticky pads to a timber batten screwed to the floor beneath the bath. The bottom of the panel is also held to the batten with raised-head chrome screws in screw cups for extra security. If an end panel is required, this fixes in a similar way, before the side panel is fitted.

Effective bath panels with recesses for shampoo bottles and so on can be made from chipboard which can later be tiled to match the walls. In this case a simple framework from 50 mm × 25 mm battens can be made under the bath rim to which the chipboard can be attached. A similar framework can be used if panels are being made from enamelled hardboard. In the latter case, finish the edge at the

corner where the side panel joins with the end panel by gluing on a strip of stainless steel or polished aluminium angle.

1. Plastic bath panels usually fit between a batten screwed to the floor and are held at the top by plastic clips that slot into the bath frame. The vertical batten shown screwed to the wall helps to steady the plastic bath.
2. This cross-section shows how the plastic clip holds the top of the panel against the inside edge of the bath rim while the bottom of the panel rests agains the floor batten.
3. Detail of the corner of a bath showing how clips on the edge of the end panel locate into the edge of the side panel moulding.
4. This detail shows a method of making a bath panel from chipboard which can be finished by tiling if required. Use 19 mm chipboard screwed to a 25 mm by 50 mm timber framework.
5. A simple 25 mm by 50 mm timber framework which could be covered with decorated hardboard panels, plastic laminate on chipboard, or plain chipboard for tiling. The framework is simply butt-jointed and held with corrugated timber fasteners.
6. Cross section showing how a bath rim can be double-sealed with silicone mastic against a wall. Sealant is applied first when the bath is fitted and again after wall tiles have been fixed.
7. Another point where water can enter and set up unpleasant smells is between the washbasin and pedestal. Seal this joint with silicone sealant

Index